Institutional Adaptation and Innovation in Rural Mexico

The Transformation of Rural Mexico Series, 11
Center for U.S.–Mexican Studies
University of California, San Diego

There are two companion volumes to the present book, both published by the Center for U.S.–Mexican Studies:

- The Future Role of the Ejido in Rural Mexico, *edited by Richard Snyder and Gabriel Torres* (1998)
- Strategies for Resource Management, Production, and Marketing in Rural Mexico, *edited by Guadalupe Rodríguez and Richard Snyder* (forthcoming, 1999)

Other Titles in the Series

- Rural Transformations Seen from Below: Regional and Local Perspectives from Western Mexico
- Mexican Sugarcane Growers: Economic Restructuring and Political Options
- Viva Zapata! Generation, Gender, and Historical Consciousness in the Reception of Ejido Reform in Oaxaca
- Rebellion in Chiapas: Rural Reforms, Campesino Radicalism, and the Limits to Salinismo
- Rural Reform in Mexico: The View from the Comarca Lagunera
- The End of Agrarian Reform in Mexico: Past Lessons, Future Prospects
- Economic Restructuring and Rural Subsistence in Mexico: Corn and the Crisis of the 1980s
- Mexico's Second Agrarian Reform: Household and Community Responses
- El Campo Queretano en Transición

This volume was published with the assistance of the Ford Foundation, the University of California Institute for Mexico and the United States (UC MEXUS), and the William and Flora Hewlett Foundation.

Institutional Adaptation and Innovation in Rural Mexico

edited by

Richard Snyder

LA JOLLA

CENTER FOR U.S.–MEXICAN STUDIES
UNIVERSITY OF CALIFORNIA, SAN DIEGO | LA JOLLA

Cover: Detail from a linoleum block print by Annika Nelson

Printed in the United States of America

ISBN 1-878367-41-2

Contents

Preface

Mexico's campesinos face unprecedented challenges. A 1992 constitutional amendment ending the ejido's special legal status and permitting the sale of collectively controlled lands has created new pressures for campesinos to make their production choices individually. At the same time, the withdrawal of state-owned enterprises and government subsidies from the countryside as a result of neoliberal economic reforms has forced rural producers to seek private sources of credit and reorganize their productive activities. Mexico's increasing integration into global commodity markets under the North American Free Trade Agreement (NAFTA) and the General Agreement on Tariffs and Trade (GATT) has further challenged campesinos by compelling them to find new strategies for competing in both the national and the international marketplace.

To understand how rural producers have adapted to these dramatic changes, the Center for U.S.–Mexican Studies, in association with the Centro de Investigaciones y Estudios Superiores en Antropología Social de Occidente (CIESAS–Occidente), launched a multidisciplinary research project on "The Transformation of Rural Mexico: Building an Economically Viable and Participatory Campesino Sector." The project, which was carried out in 1996 and 1997, sought to identify the key factors that help or hinder campesino-led efforts to achieve socially equitable, participatory development. The project was primarily supported by a grant to the Center for U.S.–Mexican Studies from the Ford Foundation through its office for Mexico and Central America. Additional funding was provided by a grant from the University of California Institute for Mexico and the United States (UC MEXUS).

Together with CIESAS–Occidente, the Center for U.S.–Mexican Studies organized an international research team of twenty-two scholars based at institutions in Mexico and the United States. Project participants carried out collaborative field research and collected fresh data with the goal of illuminating the on-the-ground consequences of the current reforms. In order to situate their empirical findings in a coherent analytic framework, project members focused on three priority research areas: the future role of the ejido in rural society and politics; institutional adaptation and innovation; and strategies for production, marketing, and resource management. These three areas form a core agenda for scholars and policy makers seeking to understand the broad economic, social, political, and environmental consequences of dramatic changes in rural Mexico.

Participants in the project carried out field research in the summer and fall of 1996 and presented their findings and policy recommendations at an international conference in Guadalajara, Mexico, in April 1997. This volume consists of expanded and significantly revised versions of papers on institutional adaptation and innovation presented at the Guadalajara conference. Papers focusing on the transformation of the ejido were published previously in *The Future Role of the Ejido in Rural Mexico*, edited by Richard Snyder and Gabriel Torres (Center for U.S.–Mexican Studies, 1998). A third volume on strategies for production, marketing, and resource management will be published later this year, also by the Center for U.S.–Mexican Studies.

1

Patterns of Institutional Change in Rural Mexico

Richard Snyder

The 1990s was a period of dramatic change in rural Mexico. The decade began with the implementation of a massive program of market-oriented, or neoliberal, economic reforms. This policy shift resulted in the dismantling of state-owned enterprises and the withdrawal of government subsidies from the countryside. In 1992, a constitutional amendment ended the ejido's special legal status and permitted the sale of collectively controlled lands, creating new pressures for campesinos to make their production choices individually. Moreover, the Mexican government's policy of pursing greater integration into global commodity markets through the North American Free Trade Agreement (NAFTA) and the World Trade Organization (WTO) challenged rural producers to devise new strategies for competing in both the national and the international marketplace.

The contributors to this volume explore the complex processes of institutional transformation unleashed by these reforms. The most important finding that emerges from the essays is that instead of paving the way for triumph by free market forces, neoliberal reforms in rural Mexico triggered the construction of new institutions for market governance. The contemporary Mexican countryside is not a barren wasteland ruled by unregulated market forces. Rather, it is a rich, complex landscape with different types of institutions for market governance that connect producer organizations, government actors, and private firms in novel and often surprising ways.

This finding casts the transformations of the past decade in a new light. Instead of viewing the 1990s as a purely destructive episode dominated by institutional retrenchment and dismantling, this period should also be seen as a creative episode of institutional reconstruction and innovation. Instead of focusing on how the old institutions of statism were dismantled, students of rural Mexico should shift their attention to understanding the new institutions that have replaced those destroyed or displaced by the neoliberal reforms. The essays in this volume take an important step in that direction.

Institutional Reconstruction after Neoliberalism: Sectoral Perspectives

One fruitful strategy for understanding institutional innovation in rural Mexico focuses on the effects of neoliberal reforms in a particular economic sector. The chapters by Mackinlay and Snyder, which analyze the tobacco and coffee sectors, respectively, provide two contrasting perspectives on the kinds of new institutions that can result after the implementation of neoliberal reforms.

Mackinlay analyzes how the dismantling of a state-owned company, Tabacos Mexicanos, S.A. de C.V. (TABAMEX), transformed the tobacco sector. His study shows that the withdrawal of a federal government enterprise can result in a situation of unmediated, bipartite exchange relationships between small producers and private agroindustrial firms. The chapter explores how these bipartite relationships take distinct forms depending on the strength and strategies of producer organizations. Where small tobacco farmers lacked strong organizations, they were forced into individualized relationships with private companies that required them to bargain alone. By contrast, where the small farmers had powerful unions, they were able to bargain collectively with the companies and could therefore secure more equitable contracts. An especially intriguing finding concerns how cross-regional variations in the style and intensity of TABAMEX's intervention had an enduring impact on the fortunes of small producer organizations, an influence that persisted well after the demise of the state-owned enterprise. Furthermore, local differences in the *terms* of TABAMEX's withdrawal—for example, how much and what kind of infrastructure it transferred to producers—also had an important impact on the subsequent capacities of producer organizations.

Snyder's analysis of the coffee sector provides a strikingly different perspective on the consequences of neoliberal reforms. His study shows that the dismantling of a federal government enterprise does not necessarily lead to a direct, bipartite exchange relationship between small producers and large private firms, as occurred in the tobacco sector. Rather, *state* governments can take control of policy areas abandoned by the federal government, a process that can result in new kinds of *tripartite* institutions at the subnational level that coordinate the activities of government, small producers, and private firms.

Politicians face strong incentives to attempt to reregulate rural markets. If their reregulation projects are challenged by powerful grassroots organizations, the outcome may be a participatory policy regime that helps improve the welfare of small farmers. Snyder develops this argument by focusing on the case of Oaxaca, where the dismantling of the Mexican Coffee Institute (INMECAFÉ) resulted in new, participatory institutions for coordinating public policy at the state level. These institutions greatly strengthened the ability of Oaxaca's small coffee farmers to compete in the international marketplace.

The chapters by Mackinlay and Snyder also offer important insights about the different ways that rural production processes can be reorganized after the implementation of neoliberal reforms. The case of tobacco illustrates how such reforms can result in a production regime that allows small farmers very little control over the production process. Mackinlay shows that, regardless of whether or not producers were well organized, the private tobacco firms controlled marketing and the allocation of credit, inputs, and technology packages after the dismantling of TABAMEX. Consequently, producers could do little more than produce; that is, they could only grow and harvest tobacco. The most lucrative stage of the production process— marketing—was out of their control.

The alternative scenario is seen in the case of coffee, where the dismantling of INMECAFÉ resulted in a new production regime that allowed small farmers far more control over financing and marketing. After INMECAFÉ withdrew, small producers in Oaxaca and other coffee-producing states made considerable advances in their efforts to "appropriate" the production process by taking direct control of profitable activities such as marketing.

The structure of production regimes matters because the welfare of small producers often hinges on how much control they have over the production process. Furthermore, the type of production regime can have a decisive impact on the kinds of roles available to producer organizations, a factor that strongly influences the sustainability of such organizations. In the case of tobacco, because private companies firmly controlled marketing as well as the allocation of credit, inputs, and technology packages, the scope of feasible activities that producer organizations could carry out was restricted to securing higher prices and negotiating contracts with the companies. In the case of coffee, by contrast, producer organizations faced a far less constraining production regime and were therefore able to undertake a much broader range of activities, often operating as full-fledged campesino enterprises.

Between the extremes of extensive producer control over the production process, as in coffee, and minimal producer control, as in tobacco, a wide range of intermediate scenarios is possible. Future research should aim to achieve a stronger understanding of the factors that explain the contrasting production regimes that result after the implementation of neoliberal reforms. The evidence in this volume highlights the important role that government actors can play in shaping post-neoliberal production regimes. The capacity of Oaxaca's small coffee producers to move into activities like financing, processing, and marketing was strengthened in crucial ways by state and federal government programs. By contrast, such government programs were strikingly absent in the case of tobacco.

New Sizes and Roles for Campesino Organizations

The policy reforms of the last decade have exposed campesinos to new competitive pressures in both the national and the international marketplace. How have campesino organizations responded to these challenges? The contributors to this volume highlight two divergent trends: some organizations have pursued a strategy of miniaturization and "scaling down" that involves reducing the size of the membership; others, by contrast, have pursued a strategy of "scaling up" that involves increasing the size of the membership.

The chapter by Soto Romero on fishing and credit cooperatives in Baja California illustrates the advantages of scaling down. Soto Romero analyzes two very successful micro-cooperatives with approximately twenty-five members each. The study shows how these micro-cooperatives were able to draw on social capital—that is, dense parochial ties, strong associational networks, and deep interpersonal trust—to help lower the costs of doing business. Soto Romero's analysis also suggests that micro-cooperatives may be able to organize and thrive even in contexts where the initial supply of social capital is small. Appropriate and enforceable formal rules for governing a cooperative can compensate for a limited supply of social capital and potentially can help foster the accumulation of such capital. Where the amount of social capital is small, well-crafted formal rules make cooperation easier, and cooperation, in turn, can increase the supply of social capital. Soto Romero's analysis of the VIC-TOR cooperative offers a vivid illustration of how effective formal rules can trigger such a process of cascading cooperation.

The important role of local, parochial ties in strengthening producer organizations is also evident in the chapter by Hernández Díaz, which shows how shared ethnic and linguistic bonds contributed to the success of coffee producer cooperatives in the Chatino region of

Oaxaca. Hernández Díaz uncovers an intriguing feedback process whereby the participation of the Chatino farmers in formal producer organizations actually helped strengthen and consolidate their shared ethnic identity.

Despite the potential advantages of miniaturization, the evidence in this volume also suggests that small is not necessarily better: scaling down involves important costs. Although micro-organizations rooted in strong parochial ties often face lower transaction costs than do larger organizations, miniaturization can nevertheless result in a loss of economies of scale. This trade-off between reducing transaction costs, on the one hand, and achieving economies of scale, on the other, provides a plausible basis for making an efficiency-based argument in favor of big campesino organizations. The value of economies of scale can be seen clearly in the chapter by Guerrero Anaya. His study highlights the impressive achievements of a peasant-owned agro-industrial enterprise, the Western Agricultural Marketing Company (COMAGRO), which has a broad membership base spread across five states.

Moreover, large-scale organizations can have distinct advantages over micro-organizations in the political arena. Snyder's chapter illustrates the potential political rewards of scaling up. He shows how a widespread federation of local and regional producer organizations, the Statewide Coordinating Network of Coffee Producers of Oaxaca (CEPCO), was able to launch a successful challenge to the governor of Oaxaca's exclusionary, neocorporatist project, thereby contributing to the construction of participatory institutions for market governance that improved the welfare of small coffee producers. Had Oaxaca's producer organizations been micro-cooperatives of the kind analyzed by Soto Romero, they would have lacked the political clout necessary to achieve a participatory institutional outcome.

Although the notable achievements of COMAGRO and CEPCO do suggest the advantages of scaling up, it bears emphasis that both organizations were federations of multiple smaller-scale organizations. And these smaller organizations were often anchored in precisely the kinds of parochial ties highlighted by Soto Romero and Hernández Díaz. This observation raises the intriguing possibility that a widespread federation of locally rooted organizations may be an especially effective organizational format because it can combine the strengths of large and small organizations.

In addition to experimenting with new sizes, Mexico's campesino organizations are also exploring new roles.[1] The evidence in this vol-

---

[1] The issues of the appropriate sizes and roles for Mexico's campesino organizations are closely intertwined, because an organization's size may have a decisive impact on the kinds of roles available to it.

ume illustrates a variety of such roles, ranging from: (1) *withdrawal from production* accompanied by a focus on collective bargaining with private firms and/or government (for example, the tobacco producer organizations of the Nayarit-Jalisco zone analyzed by Mackinlay); (2) a *thin productivist* role restricted to marketing crops and inputs and, by extension, to price regulation (for example, COMAGRO as analyzed by Guerrero Anaya); (3) a *thick productivist* role that includes collective management of credit and crop processing in addition to joint marketing of crops and inputs (for example, the coffee producer organizations analyzed by Snyder and Hernández Díaz, as well as the micro-cooperatives analyzed by Soto Romero); and (4) a *full-service* role that encompasses not only a broad range of production-related activities but also nutritional, health, and basic consumption needs (for example, the Independent Peasant Organization of Jalisco "Manuel Ramírez" [OCIJ] analyzed by Guerrero Anaya).

What roles or combinations of roles are most appropriate for Mexico's campesino organizations? The contributors offer some tentative answers to this important question. In his analysis of several of the medium-sized campesino organizations affiliated with COMAGRO, Guerrero Anaya argues that they should move beyond merely selling crops. According to Guerrero Anaya, such organizations need to thicken their roles by expanding into activities that help campesinos achieve increases in productivity. Mackinlay makes a similar argument by highlighting the limitations of a major producer organization that focused narrowly on securing higher tobacco prices. On the other hand, taking on too many new functions too quickly can overextend the capabilities of an organization and lead to disaster. Campesino organizations will thus need to find a balance between expanding into new activities and specializing in areas where they can make the greatest contribution to the welfare of their members.

Another important issue concerns the future status of officially sponsored organizations affiliated with the Institutional Revolutionary Party's (PRI) corporatist peasant unions. The chapters by Hernández Díaz and Mackinlay focus on organizations affiliated with the PRI's National Peasants' Confederation (CNC). Their analyses suggest important questions for subsequent research. What future do CNC–affiliated unions have in a democratic Mexico where the old concepts of "official" and "independent" will increasingly lose their meaning? How have CNC organizations adapted to the growing number of situations where opposition political parties control state and/or local government? As the hegemony of the ruling PRI continues to weaken, will CNC organizations disappear? Or, alternatively, will the solidarities forged under the aegis of the old PRI regime endure and exert an ongoing influence across rural Mexico? Because literally hundreds of thousands of campesinos have belonged to officially sponsored organizations, addressing questions such as these should be considered an important priority for future research.

Conclusion

The essays in this volume highlight how the legacies of past policies influence the outcomes of subsequent ones. Decades of statist intervention in the Mexican countryside profoundly altered the terrain on which the neoliberal policy reforms of the 1990s were implemented. One of the strongest aspects of the statist legacy has been the sustained presence of both official campesino organizations nurtured by the state itself and independent organizations that initially formed to challenge the state's role. These collective actors have often acquired a vibrant life of their own that has enabled them to survive into the post-statist period. Because of enduring legacies such as these, the implementation of neoliberal policies and the withdrawal of the state have not automatically revived the pre-statist status quo, a period characterized by disorganized producers at the mercy of a long chain of middlemen. Instead, as the contributors to this volume show, the neoliberal reforms have resulted in a diverse array of new economic institutions that connect producer organizations, government actors, and private firms in a variety of ways.

In addition to legacies such as these, the prior episode of statist policies has also had an enduring cognitive impact on rural actors. This impact can be seen in the many examples of *learning* analyzed in this volume. For example, Soto Romero's chapter shows how the founders of new micro-cooperatives benefited from the negative lessons about what *not* to do that they acquired through their previous experiences with the old, leviathan CNC unions. Similarly, Snyder's analysis suggests that their prior experiences with exclusionary corporatist institutions helped Oaxaca's small coffee farmers learn how to achieve a new, welfare-enhancing kind of corporatism that fostered participatory coordination of economic policy.

Taken together, the findings that neoliberal reforms do not necessarily revive the pre-statist status quo and that past policies can stimulate learning and experimentation underscore the importance of viewing the 1990s as a period of institutional reconstruction and innovation. The contributors to this volume have taken an important first step toward helping us understand the different kinds of new institutions that have replaced those destroyed by neoliberal reforms. The next step is to extend these efforts.

2

Institutional Transformation in the Tobacco Sector: Collective or Individualized Bargaining?

Horacio Mackinlay

The withdrawal of the state from the rural arena during the first half of the 1990s had important repercussions in the Mexican countryside. Previously, a number of large state-owned companies dominated the rural economy, some regulating the market for basic food products, others providing subsidized agricultural inputs, and still others intervening in the production and marketing of particular commercial crops. These institutions were key economic actors; they were key political and social actors as well. As a result of the dismantling of these state-owned enterprises, campesino organizations have undergone profound transformations. In some cases they have survived; in others they have disappeared or been transformed into new and different organizations.

Because of the economic importance of products such as coffee, sugarcane, and tobacco, and the large number of small farmers involved in their cultivation, these crops received special attention from the Mexican government, which has always understood their strategic significance for maintaining political control in the countryside. During the 1970s, government-controlled corporatist unions representing coffee, sugarcane, and tobacco producers became pillars of the "official" National Peasants' Confederation (CNC) (Mackinlay

---

Translation by Patricia Rosas.

1996). The corporatist unions were tightly linked to the state-owned companies that intervened in the production and marketing of these three strategic crops. Producers affiliated with these unions enjoyed a series of benefits, such as inscription in the Mexican Social Security Institute (IMSS), and profit margins considerably higher than those found in the cultivation of crops not subject to such direct state control.

In the tobacco sector in the late 1970s, during the period of greatest expansion of the state-owned company, Tabacos Mexicanos, S.A. de C.V. (TABAMEX), there were approximately 16,000 tobacco farmers in the Nayarit–Jalisco zone and approximately 14,000 in the Gulf zone (the states of Veracruz, Oaxaca, and Chiapas) (Teubal et al. 1982: 47).[1] Tobacco employs a high proportion of salaried workers in both cultivation and processing activities, generating a significant economic effect in the regions where it is grown and creating employment in industrial and commercial activities related to the cigarette industry. Additionally, tobacco exports bring in foreign exchange, and cigarette taxes are an important revenue source for the Mexican government.

The dismantling of TABAMEX resulted in the emergence of a variety of new institutional arrangements across Mexico's tobacco-growing regions. In the Nayarit–Jalisco zone, a regional-level collective bargaining framework was established with a single organization representing all area farmers. In the Gulf zone, by contrast, the dismantling of TABAMEX produced a range of results, from the extinction of tobacco cultivation in the state of Oaxaca and a dramatic decline in its importance in the northern part of Veracruz, to the destruction of the collective bargaining framework in Chiapas. If there is a commonality between the Nayarit–Jalisco and Gulf zones, it is that control of tobacco production has been transferred, with few exceptions, to large national and transnational private companies, despite an initial proposal to have campesino organizations play a central role in the production process.

Since the dismantling of TABAMEX, campesinos in the tobacco sector have seen their role limited to negotiating contracts directly with private companies, without the involvement of the state.[2] They

---

[1] This geographical distribution corresponds to the operational and administrative subdivisions of TABAMEX. The Nayarit–Jalisco zone includes a tobacco-growing belt in Jalisco that borders on Nayarit, but Jalisco's overall contribution to tobacco production, even in the best of times, has not exceeded 3 percent of total national output.

[2] In other sectors, such as coffee, campesino organizations were able to take control of the assets of the old state-owned companies and to form their own enterprises and trade links, including, in some cases, with the international market (see the chapters

do so either collectively through representation by a campesino organization or on an individual basis, with just one farmer or a small
group of farmers taking part. In both situations, instead of three actors—the campesinos, the state, and the private companies—as before, there are only two parties to the negotiation: the campesinos and
the companies. This new bargaining context in the tobacco sector is
an important sign that the corporatist institutions that characterized
Mexico's agrarian reform period (1917–1992) are undergoing profound transformations which need to be analyzed in depth.

The following section provides an overview of the sector and dis-
cusses the specific characteristics of tobacco cultivation, a necessary
background to understanding what follows. The third section examines the dismantling of TABAMEX, a process that laid the groundwork
for a new role for campesino organizations. The fourth part analyzes
how campesino organizations in the Nayarit–Jalisco zone have responded to TABAMEX's withdrawal. The penultimate section explores
the varied consequences of TABAMEX's dismantling in the Gulf zone.

This chapter seeks to improve our understanding of these transformations by focusing on campesino organizations in the state of
Nayarit after the withdrawal of TABAMEX. The chapter also incorpo-
rates comparisons with the tobacco-growing regions in coastal Chiapas and in northern and southern Veracruz. After an examination of
the restructuring process that the tobacco agro-industry underwent
from the days of state intervention to those of private control of the
production process, the chapter turns to its main objective: analyzing
the new forms of bargaining that have emerged between campesinos
and private companies, as well as the social impacts of these arrangements.

Overview of the Tobacco Sector

The tobacco industry has been important in Mexico since the second
half of the nineteenth century. At that time, principally in the states of
Veracruz, Tabasco, Oaxaca, Yucatán, and Chiapas, the cultivation of
dark tobaccos used in cigars predominated. The second decade of the
twentieth century saw the appearance of a mass market for cigarettes
made from blond tobacco leaf. These light tobaccos, produced in a
mechanized manner, were well suited to the soils on the coast of
Nayarit, and their cultivation soon spread at an amazing rate. In

by Snyder and Hernández Díaz, in this volume). In the tobacco sector, this occurred
in only two instances, discussed in the section on Veracruz.

1930, Nayarit already accounted for 52 percent of all tobacco produced in Mexico and 42 percent of the total area cultivated in that crop. By the 1980s, Nayarit contained more than 80 percent of Mexico's total area cultivated in tobacco, and the state was producing a similar percentage of Mexico's overall tobacco output (TABAMEX 1989: 43, 105, 107).

The British and North American cigarette companies that pioneered the use of light tobacco for cigarettes also introduced the practice of contract agriculture, a system especially suited to crops where the buyer needs a product with standardized qualities. Under a contract system, cigarette company representatives provide financing, technical assistance, and the technological package—all of which the small farmers cannot afford—and by doing so, the companies ensure uniformity in the crop. In the contracts, the price for the final product is established in advance, and the farmer is required not to produce more than was stipulated, to accept whatever inspections are considered necessary, and to sell his product exclusively to the company with which he has signed the agreement. At the end of the season, a settlement is made to the farmer based on the sale price of the tobacco, less the value of the loan the farmer received from the company during the agricultural season. Thus the season-end settlement is the profit that the farmer earns each year.[3]

The cigarette companies lend a complete credit and technology package that includes both inputs (seedlings, fertilizers, herbicides, insecticides, and so forth) and cash (to cover the wages of farmworkers and the cost of farm services such as irrigation or machinery rentals). Because campesino tobacco growers usually rely on household labor, at the end of the season the farmer is able to keep, in addition to the season-end settlement, funds allocated as wages for the farmworkers. If, additionally, a campesino owns irrigation equipment, farm machinery, or agricultural implements, he can also earn the amount stipulated in the contract to cover provision of these services.

The participation of the campesino is not limited to tobacco cultivation alone; it also involves post-harvest tasks, such as drying or curing the leaf, a process that is done on the farmer's own parcel using wooden drying sheds (*galeras*), large metal sheds (*galerones*), or simply by drying the leaf in the open air (in *sartas*). Once the tobacco is cured, the campesinos deliver their production to the companies.

---

[3] Regionally, the tobacco season begins in October and ends in June, but it takes individual farmers no more than six months to complete production work on their parcels.

(The only exception to this pattern involves the Virginia Hornos variety of tobacco, which requires curing in ovens in huge factories.) The final stage of processing consists of deveining the leaf and preparing it for storage, a process that takes place in factories with industrial workers.

Led since the 1940s by Tabaco en Rama, S.A. (TERSA), a subsidiary of the transnational corporation British American Tobacco Company, a total of six large companies were offering contract agriculture programs in Mexico by the 1960s. Four of them were subsidiaries of cigarette companies, and the remaining two produced processed tobacco for export. In light of the agrarian reform of the 1940s, which established ejidos in most of Nayarit's coastal plain, the companies designed a system of guarantees to circumvent the laws that impeded them, in case of a default by a farmer, from seizing ejidal lands in compensation for their lost investment. The system was based on "solidarity groups," or groups of "common responsibility," formed within an ejido. "In the case of losses by any given ejidatario," the other members of the group "were obliged to respond by indemnifying the debt" (Valtierra Pacheco 1984: 96). This scheme extended to all regions; but given that tobacco remained a highly profitable crop until the end of the 1960s, it was generally unnecessary to resort to the mechanism of solidarity groups to recoup financial losses.

While TERSA operated, contracts were also made with midsize and large producers, yet most tobacco farmers in Mexico were ejidatarios with only small parcels of land. Due to the advantages and relatively high profits that resulted from the tobacco credit and technology package, campesinos had strong incentives to farm that crop. The CNC, which had been advocating for the formation of a centralized entity to deal with the most important matters concerning the sector, finally achieved its goal in 1966 with the creation of the National Tobacco Council (Comité Nacional del Tabaco), comprising representatives from the tobacco companies, the federal Ministry of Agriculture, the governments of tobacco-producing states, and the campesino organizations. The council's goal was to resolve an array of issues facing the tobacco sector and to review pricing on a yearly basis. The council negotiated certain agreements, such as limiting contracts with ejidatarios to cover an area of no more than 4 hectares and contracts with private smallholders to cover an area of no more than 12 hectares, in order to avoid the concentration of tobacco credits in the hands of large producers. Nevertheless, most agreements were never respected. Despite increases in cigarette prices authorized in 1967 and again in 1971, the cigarette companies refused to increase the price they paid for tobacco during that period (Bonfil 1986: 154).

The parastatal TABAMEX was founded in November 1972, in the context of President Luis Echeverría's (1970–1976) populist and statist policies. One of the factors influencing the formation of TABAMEX was farmers' increasing dismay over their deteriorating relationship with the companies that provided the credit and technology packages and over the absence of channels through which to make their demands heard. Another was the need to protect the farmers from the monopolistic powers of TERSA, which could easily collude with the few other companies on prices, lending practices, and other issues relevant to the tobacco agro-industry. In effect, the control that the transnational companies had over the production chain was total.[4] It began with cultivation and post-harvest activities and continued all the way through the manufacture and export of cigarettes. Blocked from seeking alternatives because of the lack of competition among the companies, tobacco farmers had little leverage with which to defend their interests.

TABAMEX was formed with three categories of shareholders: 52 percent belonged to the federal government, 24 percent to the cigarette companies, and 24 percent to the CNC and the organized tobacco producers, as stipulated in the presidential decree that created it (Chumacero 1986: 211). The four cigarette companies, which initially held the shares corresponding to the private sector, quickly merged so that by the mid–1970s only two remained, Cigarrera La Moderna and Cigarrera La Tabacalera Mexicana (Cigatam). The first was owned by the British American Tobacco Company, and the second was a partner of Philip Morris International.[5]

Before the start of the agricultural cycle, the private companies negotiated with TABAMEX over the number of hectares to be planted and the varieties of tobacco they would buy, and they were involved in setting tobacco prices and determining the value of the credit and technology package. Most importantly, the private companies advanced TABAMEX the working capital it required to finance the harvest, and they established a system for overseeing cultivation, which operated independently of controls implemented by the parastatal. In this way, the state-owned company became an intermediary between

[4] Currently, only six large transnational corporations control an important fraction of the international tobacco trade (see Malo Juvera Castañeda 1996: 49–64).

[5] TABAMEX itself acquired 60 percent of the shares of the two privately owned deveining and export companies installed in Nayarit, while the remaining 40 percent stayed under the control of their previous owners. These two companies were Extamex (Exportación de Tabacos Mexicanos), a subsidiary of K. R. Edwards Leaf Tobacco, and Tabacos Aztecas, a subsidiary of the Austin Company.

the tobacco farmers, on the one side, and the two large cigarette companies and the two remaining exporters, on the other. During the 1980s, Cigarrera La Moderna and Cigatam were bought out by two large Mexican industrial conglomerates, Grupo Pulsar and Grupo Carso.[6] These two conglomerates formed a duopoly that dominated the cigarette industry; together they had cornered 99 percent of the national cigarette market. (The remaining 1 percent was covered by a small company called La Libertad.)

During the 1980s, 73 percent of Mexico's national tobacco production, on average, supplied the domestic market, with the remaining 27 percent being exported (although the volume exported fluctuated markedly from year to year) (see Saldívar Von Wuthenau 1991: 161).[7] A relatively small amount of the tobacco needed for Mexican domestic cigarette blends was regularly imported, but at times—mainly when natural disaster struck—larger quantities of tobacco were imported. During the period of TABAMEX's existence, contracts were limited to 4 hectares, a limitation applicable to both ejidatarios and private smallholders. The purpose of this limitation was to make the tobacco credit and technology package available to more campesinos.[8] An additional feature is that 97 percent of the tobacco farmers listed on the rosters of the parastatal were ejidatarios (Giarracca 1983: 140).

As a company, TABAMEX earned profits that it reinvested in order to carry out its functions, among which was agro-technological research. But its actions were not always taken in accord with strict standards of good business practice because the company also responded to pressing political and social issues. In fact, as time passed, increased levels of administrative inefficiency and corruption provoked an alarming decline in product quality and contributed to income losses for the parastatal. Despite that, until 1986 TABAMEX was classified as financially sound, although it was only able to record a profit because it was inserted in a highly profitable market. Begin-

---

[6] For more information on these industrial groups, see La Moderna 1996; *Business Week*, March 1, 1996, and *Proceso*, November 24, 1996.

[7] The North American Free Trade Agreement (NAFTA) will help increase the volume of exports of processed tobacco leaf; but it does not change the situation in the cigarette market because the companies have agreements that regulate the exportation of franchised brands. The Mexican cigarette companies, especially Cigarrera La Moderna, focus their energies on exporting their brands outside North America (see Malo Juvera Castañeda 1996: chap. 5).

[8] The only exception was in regard to Burley tobacco, grown for the export market, whose limit was set at 5 hectares because of the scarcity of land appropriate for its cultivation.

ning in 1987, it began to operate in the red which, according to a proponent of privatization, meant it was no longer cost effective to keep
it in operation (Saldívar Von Wuthenau 1991: 112–21). The dismantling process began in late 1989, in the context of an aggressive neoliberal program of privatization of state-owned enterprises implemented by the administration of President Carlos Salinas de Gortari
(1988–1994).

The Dismantling of TABAMEX: New Roles for Producer Organizations

During the first two years of the Salinas administration, Gustavo
Gordillo, undersecretary for social policy within the Ministry of Agriculture (SARH), was in charge of the restructuring and divestment
processes for most parastatals involved in the rural sector. Gordillo
deviated from neoliberal orthodoxy by promoting the "autonomy of
the producer" through government-assisted "appropriation of the
production process." One method for achieving this appropriation
consisted of giving priority, in the transfer of a parastatal's infrastructure, to campesino organizations that had the ability to manage it effectively.[9] Nevertheless, as had also been the case with Azúcar S.A.
de C.V., the parastatal that owned most of Mexico's sugarmills, the
privatization of TABAMEX was, in fact, orchestrated from the offices of
Luis Téllez, undersecretary for planning within the SARH. Téllez
supported orthodox neoliberal reforms and represented the interests
of those favoring the business sector. He was later one of the main
promoters of the 1992 rural reform legislation that would lead to the
privatization of the ejido.

The dismantling of TABAMEX, announced in October 1989 and
concluded in September 1990, consisted of selling or transferring infrastructure related to the cultivation and marketing of processed
tobacco to private companies and campesino organizations. Others
could take part in auctions of certain assets that were not essential to
tobacco production. The privatization strategy, approved at the highest government levels, called for designing a new market framework
for the tobacco sector.[10] Nevertheless, like many activities in which

---

[9] This was part of a broader platform of "renewal of the state-campesino alliance" promoted by Salinas during his presidential campaign. For more information, see De la
Fuente and Mackinlay 1994.

[10] Information on the TABAMEX privatization is not readily available. Fortunately, Juan
Saldívar Von Wuthenau, an official in the Ministry of Agriculture who participated in

diverse interests and many different actors take part, the outcome was very different from what had been intended.

The initial plan was based on the premise that it was necessary to liquidate an economically unviable parastatal, one that operated inefficiently because it was overly protective of the farmers' interests. From this premise came the notion of returning to the direct buyer-seller relationship that had governed producers' relations with cigarette companies and exporters prior to the creation of TABAMEX. On the other hand, the cigarette industry, by virtue of being made up of a few large business groups, was a potential oligopoly, and for that reason it was deemed unwise to abruptly open the sector to unfettered market forces. A better course, it was thought, would be a gradual move toward the free market. That is, it was necessary to avoid the creation of a new "monopoly of buyers" that would recreate the situation that had prevailed when TERSA had dominated the sector before the creation of TABAMEX. During that period, so the argument went, given the weakness of the farmers (who were unorganized and had scant negotiating power), TERSA had completely ignored the campesinos' "urgent demands," which, in turn, generated the very frictions that had led to the creation of TABAMEX (Saldívar Von Wuthenau 1991: 46–50).

Contrary to what one would assume, given that the plan was implemented by a team dominated by pro-neoliberal technocrats, the first thoughts about how to privatize did not strictly follow neoliberal orthodoxy. Even though at heart the privatization initiative was predominantly pro-business, the project could not entirely ignore the contemporary official rural-sector policies of Mexico's government as outlined in the 1989–1994 National Modernization Plan and the 1990–1994 National Program for Rural Modernization, which were profoundly influenced by Gordillo's unorthodox point of view. Leaving aside whether common ground may have been negotiated between the two camps in the Salinas administration, or whether the proposal expressed what the Téllez team may have really believed to be appropriate at that time, in concrete terms the initial plan to dismantle TABAMEX contained the following steps:

- The farmers would receive assets "used in the production and curing of tobacco," which would include "tools for planting,

---

the development of the privatization scheme for the parastatal, wrote a thesis on the subject (1991). Even though the thesis was completed before the process ended, it contains valuable information and represents the version that comes closest to the "official source."

FIGURE 2.1

CHANGING PRODUCTION REGIMES IN THE MEXICAN TOBACCO SECTOR

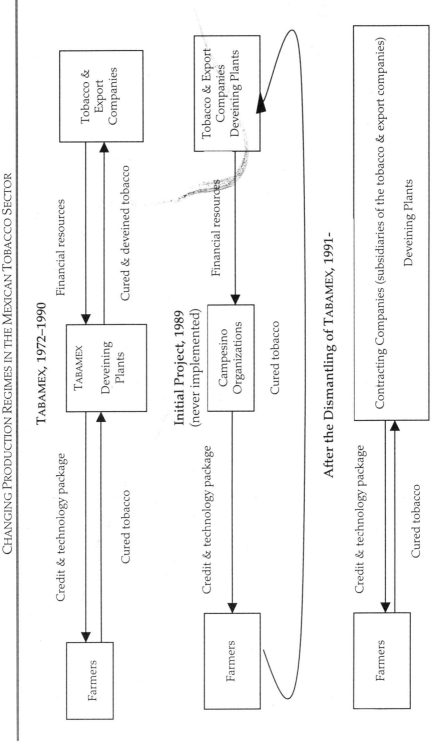

TABAMEX, 1972–1990

Farmers → Credit & technology package → TABAMEX Deveining Plants
TABAMEX Deveining Plants → Cured tobacco → Farmers
TABAMEX Deveining Plants → Financial resources → Tobacco & Export Companies
Tobacco & Export Companies → Cured & deveined tobacco → TABAMEX Deveining Plants

Initial Project, 1989 (never implemented)

Farmers → Credit & technology package → Campesino Organizations
Campesino Organizations → Cured tobacco → Farmers
Campesino Organizations → Financial resources → Tobacco & Export Companies Deveining Plants

After the Dismantling of TABAMEX, 1991-

Farmers → Credit & technology package → Contracting Companies (subsidiaries of the tobacco & export companies) Deveining Plants
Contracting Companies → Cured tobacco → Farmers

sowing, and harvesting, transportation equipment, ovens, drying sheds, warehouses, and 5 percent of the shares of the deveining plants."

- "The remaining stages in the process (deveining, distribution, production of seedlings, research, financing, and so on) must be covered by the industry." Thus "the respective parties will have complete control over the activities that each acquires, [with sufficient] freedom to act and the possibility of substantially increasing their incomes and standards of living."

- In order to regulate relations among the different actors in the sector, a tobacco regulatory committee was to be created—comprising representatives of the federal government, the affected state governments, the farmers, and the industrialists. Its objectives would be to (1) act as "arbiter in the setting of prices according to the type and quality of the tobacco, taking international prices as a reference point," (2) assist with the distribution of "import licenses according to production and domestic prices," (3) oversee the "fulfillment of contracts between producers and buyers," and (4) avoid overly abrupt fluctuations in the size of the area cultivated and in the number of contracted farmers. This committee would be temporary, and it was understood that the government would withdraw from it within a period of approximately ten years (Saldívar Von Wuthenau 1991: 125–27).

- The formation of a Tobacco Institute, in which the cigarette companies would participate, would ensure the development of new technologies and the cultivation and distribution of seedlings, among other functions.

Let us now review the results of the divestment process and identify the problems that prevented the implementation of most of these proposals (see figure 2.1). Proceeding from the last to the first item:

- The idea of a Tobacco Institute was unsound because it required the companies to support it financially, whereas each preferred to have its own independent research infrastructure. Moreover, how would the research results be shared among companies who were competitors? For these obvious reasons, the two tobacco giants in Mexico—Cigarrera La Moderna and Cigatam—did not accept the proposal, and the idea never got off the ground. Instead, each company formed its own research center, set up its own experimental fields, and jealously guarded its own company secrets.

- The tobacco regulatory committee never saw the light of day because conflicts (examined in detail below) arose before it was even formed. Nevertheless, it is interesting to note the similarity between this proposal and the one made in the 1960s for the National Tobacco Council.

- The three deveining plants that TABAMEX owned, all located in the state of Nayarit, were sold, as planned, to private companies. The largest, Lázaro Cárdenas, was purchased by Cigatam, while the government's shares in the other two were purchased by Cigarrera La Moderna.[11] No action was taken on the proposal that the organized campesinos receive 5 percent of the shares in the these plants.

- In the initial plan, campesino organizations were supposed to become micro-versions of TABAMEX, with responsibility for administering credit and producing and curing tobacco leaf.[12] The one difference was that the farmers' product would not be bought by an intermediary body; instead, the private companies, owners of the deveining plants, would purchase the leaf directly. It was also suggested that the cigarette companies advance the working capital, as had been done when TABAMEX was operating (Saldívar Von Wuthenau 1991: 125–27). Nevertheless, that idea did not have the backing of the key player—the private companies—because, in the haste to launch the plan, this issue had not been included in the negotiations with the private companies.

- The cigarette companies were relatively unconcerned about the proposal that the campesino organizations take over Tabamex assets used in the production and curing of tobacco. However, they were reluctant to continue to provide the working capital through an intermediary body, whether this was a government agency, as had previously been the case, or a campesino organization, as was now being proposed. The opposition of the cigarette companies

---

[11] Cigarrera La Moderna became the principal owner of these plants but had to associate in the deveining process with K. R. Edwards Leaf Tobacco and the Austin Company, owners of 40 percent of the shares of the Extamex and Tabacos Aztecas deveining plants, respectively.

[12] One of the alternatives, as described in an article published in *La Jornada* (September 30, 1989), suggested the formation of "*sociedades mutualistas de crédito para habilitar al productor*" (farmers' credit unions) that would guarantee the repayment of loans made by buyers. In Nayarit, apparently at the urging of the governor, people played with the idea of forming a state-level public company to be called Tabacos Nayaritas (author interview with Antonio Bassols, the official in charge of liquidating TABAMEX, March 1997).

was cemented by the fact that they considered widespread corruption to be a strong possibility. Each one of the four companies ended up forming its own firm to directly manage the credit and technology package: Tabacos Desvenados, S.A. (Tadesa) became the contracting firm under Cigatam, Agroindustrias Moderna under Cigarrera La Moderna, and the export companies Tabacos del Pacífico Norte (TPN) and Exarmex-Dimon under K. R. Edwards Leaf Tobacco Co. and the Austin Co., respectively.

- The campesino organizations in the different regions received TABAMEX's local administrative offices and real estate and—in some cases—fertilizer plants and warehouses, as well as odds and ends of equipment such as pickups, transport trucks, drying sheds, and irrigation equipment. When this infrastructure was turned over to the campesino organizations, it was already clear that they would not take over the responsibilities that had been envisioned in the government's original privatization plan.

In the end, the role of the campesino organizations became mostly limited to representing their membership vis-à-vis the private companies, while the companies resumed fulfilling the same function they had performed prior to the creation of TABAMEX: providing the credit and technology package directly to the farmers. In the absence of the envisioned regulatory committee, where the federal and state governments would have acted as arbiters, a direct relationship was established between producer organizations and the companies, without any government mediation.[13] The campesino organizations acquired a sizable debt when they purchased the liquidated assets of TABAMEX. They were supposed to repay this debt to the federal government over ten years through a system of deductions from the farmers' portion of earnings from the season-end settlements. However, the infrastructure purchased is of little use because the organization did not take over the administrative functions of providing the credit and technology package that TABAMEX once carried out. Nor will the campesino organizations have a decisive role in the production process because it is so closely tied to the provision of this credit.

In fact, given that a contract between farmers and a tobacco company is accompanied by an obligatory technology package, the companies effectively manage, directly or indirectly, the assets used in

---

[13] This is not to say that the federal and state governments do not intervene on many issues within their jurisdiction at the request of one of the parties or when questions arise that may affect local or national politics. Some examples of government intervention will be presented in the analyses of individual cases.

the production process. When individual farmers do not own tractors, irrigation equipment, or other implements, the companies may
find, when weighing costs and benefits, that it is more advantageous
to provide the farm services themselves, or they may prefer to pay a
third party for these services. Only in this latter case might they contract the services of campesino organizations or other producer associations. That is why it is highly unlikely that the campesino organizations could assume a central role in production. Furthermore, it
would be very difficult for them to engage in competition with the
tobacco companies, which are much better equipped to efficiently
manage the agricultural production process because they have the
financial resources to provide credit and make large-volume purchases and large-scale investments.

Consequently, in the production chain's new configuration, campesino organizations will find it difficult to play a relevant role in the
agricultural production process even though campesino leaders have
not given up the idea of doing so in the future. As a consultant to
Nayarit's Tobacco Producers Rural Collective Interest Association
"Constituyente Gral. Esteban Baca Calderón" (ARIC) explained:

> Supposedly, ARIC, like TABAMEX, was going to provide the
> farmers with technical assistance, inputs, and everything
> needed for the marketing and sale of tobacco. But because
> of financial considerations, the delivery of credits, technical
> assistance, and inputs has remained under the control of
> the companies. ARIC ended up acting as the agent for nego-
> tiations, social issues, and everything else relating to tobacco
> farmers. Nevertheless, ARIC may achieve something more
> than just that because it has the equipment to make fertil-
> izer and insecticide, and it has trucks to transport tobacco
> and all that sort of thing (González Castañeda 1995: 30).

In any case, the principal function of the campesino organizations,
independent of their potential efficiency or utility in the agricultural
production process, became representing the combined interests of
the farmers against the private companies. This, as we will see below,
is no small thing. It requires a great deal of dedication and may ren-
der results that could be more important in the long run than taking a
direct part in the agricultural production process.

Collective Bargaining in the Nayarit–Jalisco Zone

TABAMEX's final two years were marred by administrative cutbacks
and downsizing, along with myriad problems and conflicts among

the major actors in the tobacco sector: the cigarette companies (which questioned the government's policy and threatened to cancel their contracts with the parastatal), the producers (once the announcement of the parastatal's dismantling became official in October 1989), and the many regional and state-level interests related directly or indirectly to tobacco production. The two most significant factors during this period were the introduction of a system for grading the quality of processed tobacco at the time of its purchase and a significant decline in the area of cultivated land.

The first change was the result of an ongoing complaint on the part of the private companies over the poor quality of the tobacco they were forced to buy from TABAMEX. The companies saw this situation as the result of having a standard price for all tobacco, regardless of its condition, a practice that undermined a farmer's incentive for improving the quality of the crop. Thus it was decided that the prices paid for cured tobacco varieties would be set according to four quality levels. The second significant development was that the parcels of land eligible for government financing declined from an average total of 32,000 hectares during the first part of the 1980s to 26,440 hectares during the 1988–1989 agricultural cycle and to only 19,865 during 1989–1990 (a cycle of very low production) (see tables 2.1 and 2.2). Given that the average contract at the time was for two hectares per farmer, the number of people growing tobacco also declined—from almost 16,000 to around 13,000 and 10,000, respectively—in these two final seasons before the closure of the parastatal.[14]

This situation—coinciding with the struggle among diverse interests over how to restructure the parastatal—generated great uncertainty among farmers. They had been left without any credible information and could only react to the rumors that were coming at them from all directions. The Tobacco Producers Union of Nayarit (Unión de Productores de Tabaco del Estado de Nayarit), the CNC–affiliated organization officially recognized by TABAMEX, failed to demonstrate any initiative, and by the end of 1989 a number of independent organizations had formed to fill the vacuum. The most important of these was the Front for the Defense of Tobacco Growers (FDT), led by a prosperous farmer, José Ramón López Tirado. The FDT brought together the many tobacco farmers who were unhappy about how the privatization process was being carried out, and the organization's principal claim became its demand for indemnification for those who had lost access to the credit and technology package.

---

[14] Information gathered during fieldwork from photocopies of 1996 ARIC materials.

TABLE 2.1
AREA PLANTED IN TOBACCO, BY REGION, 1980S (HECTARES)

Year	Nayarit-Jalisco	Veracruz	Oaxaca	Chiapas	Total
1979–80	38,375	6,899	2,753	1,366	49,393
1980–81	33,906	4,625	1,584	1,122	41,237
1981–82	34,805	4,298	1,628	1,358	42,089
1982–83	31,657	4,341	899	1,560	38,457
1983–84	28,511	1,450	648	1,267	31,876
1984–85	26,841	3,297	580	2,020	32,738
1985–86	36,202	5,000	1,001	3,327	45,530
1986–87	25,136	5,254	1,019	3,852	35,261
1987–88	32,826	5,288	1,033	4,092	43,239
1988–89	26,440	3,311	0	1,613	31,364
1989–90	19,865	529	125	1,138	21,657

Source: Juan Saldívar Von Wuthenau, "La desincorporación de empresas esta-tales en México: El caso de Tabamex" (bachelor's thesis, Instituto Tec-nológico Autónomo de México, 1991), p. 156.

During the first months of 1990, the FDT held protests outside the offices of the Ministry of Finance (SHCP) in Mexico City, took over TABAMEX facilities and those of other public agencies (including the offices of SARH in Tepic, the capital of Nayarit), staged sit-ins in front of Nayarit's state house, and held demonstrations in urban centers, most importantly in the tobacco-growing districts of Las Varas and Santiago Ixcuintla. These events culminated in April 1990 with a blockade of the international highway that links Mazatlán with Guadalajara (Castellón Fonseca 1992: 44). Added to the demand for indemnification was a claim for compensation for the 24 percent of TABAMEX's shares to which the producers were supposedly enti-tled. Although this claim did not have much validity in legal terms,[15] it offered a way out of the conflict, and the federal government authorized indemnification to 17,000 farmers in Nayarit and Jalisco,

---

[15] According to Antonio Bassols, the campesino organizations had never actually con-tributed the capital to acquire 24 percent of the shares. On the other hand, the com-pany was operating at a loss, so that, in any case, the farmers would have had to provide money out of their own pockets to cover the debt left by the parastatal (author interview, March 1997).

TABLE 2.2
TOBACCO PRODUCTION, BY REGION, 1980S (TONS)

Year	Nayarit-Jalisco	Veracruz	Oaxaca	Chiapas	Experimental Fields	Total
1979–80	59,591	10,999	3,970	1,734	451	76,745
1980–81	53,673	4,195	2,332	1,598	225	62,023
1981–82	59,558	7,036	3,434	1,842	169	72,039
1982–83	43,757	8,471	2,124	2,453	27	56,832
1983–84	38,784	2,170	912	1,942	39	43,847
1984–85	39,102	4,698	1,379	3,298	124	48,601
1985–86	56,443	6,425	2,031	4,285	498	69,683
1986–87	32,896	7,896	1,840	2,007	44	44,682
1987–88	52,979	8,796	2,265	5,105	154	69,299
1988–89	47,039	4,560	0	1,754	85	53,438
1989–90	28,458	394	178	1,433	0	30,463

Source: Juan Saldívar Von Wuthenau, "La desincorporación de empresas estatales en México: El caso de Tabamex" (bachelor's thesis, Instituto Tecnológico Autónomo de México, 1991), p. 156.

including those who currently had contracts with TABAMEX and those who had had contracts in previous years.

Meanwhile, the Tobacco Producers Union was replaced by ARIC (a CNC affiliate) in order to represent the farmers of Nayarit and Jalisco. In reality, this modification amounted to no more than a change of name—the leaders of the Tobacco Producers Union had moved over to ARIC—but it was a necessary step because of a requirement that the assets of TABAMEX be turned over to a *regional* association, a qualification that the Tobacco Producers Union did not meet because it was a branch of a national-level organization (the CNC's National Union of Tobacco Producers). TABAMEX officials began to negotiate with ARIC over the transfer of the parastatal's infrastructure, despite ARIC's lack of support from the grassroots that it supposedly represented.

The state government of Nayarit also backed ARIC as it faced the challenges posed by the FDT. In the pre-privatization stage, the governor was behind the proposal that ARIC act as the administrator of the credit and technology package. If this arrangement had worked out, a regional campesino organization (ARIC) would have become an important financial power. However, when the proposal for the creation of a tobacco regulatory committee was overturned, the state government lost its potential to influence the producer-industry relationship directly. Nevertheless, given the importance of the tobacco sector in economic terms and for the political stability of Nayarit, the state government exerts a powerful influence over the ARIC leadership through regional campesino political networks.

The Social Impact of Privatization

The four years following the dismantling of TABAMEX were extremely hard on tobacco producers, and the first two were especially divisive and painful. In the first agricultural season after TABAMEX's exit (1990–1991), the area cultivated with tobacco in the Nayarit–Jalisco region tumbled from the 19,865 hectares registered in the preceding season to only 14,084 hectares, cultivated by 8,655 farmers (see tables 2.2 and 2.3; also see note 14). The major changes that were announced caused immense uncertainty among the farmers, many of whom decided to sow their fields with beans, a crop whose price outlook was good. The most disturbing issue, and one that was especially divisive in the municipality of Santiago Ixcuintla—the state's principal tobacco-growing area—is the one that largely explains farmers' indecision about signing production contracts with private companies under the new arrangements. The point of contention was the announcement that individual tobacco-drying ovens were to be constructed on the farmers' own parcels and that these new installations would replace the huge regional tobacco-drying factories that had traditionally operated. Also, there was a broad rejection of the plan to make deductions from the season-end settlements to farmers in order to cover the debt incurred in the acquisition of TABAMEX assets and membership dues in the CNC and ARIC.

Another reason for hesitancy in signing contracts was that the face value of the credit and technology package and the purchase prices set for tobacco leaf that were accorded in negotiations between the companies and ARIC were considered to be extremely low. Many farmers doubted that a profit could be made by cultivating tobacco. What would become a new norm was being put in place: prices were to be set in reference to the international market, and the value of the credit and technology package would conform strictly to the costs of production, thus making it impossible for a farmer to realize any additional income by manipulating the cash received.

Under TABAMEX, the credit and technology package was deliberately, though not officially, set at a level higher than the costs of production, a figure that supposedly was based solely on the technical requirements for successful cultivation. This arrangement helped farmers maintain their families until the season-end settlement. In reality, the "surplus" built into the payments was merely an advance that would be repaid later (Jáuregui et al. 1980: 264). However, this administrative leniency reinforced a practice that had prevailed even before TABAMEX: to siphon off part of the credit and technology package for household consumption, now often with the complicity of TABAMEX inspectors. This could be accomplished by illegally reselling a portion of the agrochemical inputs or providing fewer farm services than were stipulated in the contract. Although this might result in a poorer crop, it was possible because, when the tobacco was delivered for sale, its quality did not affect its price.

In spite of these changes, during the next season (1991–1992), 15,072 farmers signed contracts covering a total of 30,692 hectares (table 2.3; note 14). On the one hand, the experiment with beans had failed because the price of this crop fell at the end of the season. On the other hand, as a result of a decline in the number of contracts in the past season and due to competition for the best fields, the cigarette companies began to offer farmers personal loans in cash if they agreed to plant tobacco.

In the middle of the agricultural season, after the contracts were signed and the loans were delivered, storms that were part of the El Niño weather phenomenon unexpectedly battered the coast of Nayarit, destroying almost half of the tobacco crop. Partly because of climatic conditions, but also because of the new economic austerity measures taken to improve efficiency, bankruptcy swept the region. Under TABAMEX, the solidarity groups, consisting on average of ten farmers cultivating about 20 hectares, had been used solely to coordinate the delivery of the credit and technology package. Now these groups regained the function for which they had originally been designed under TERSA: campesinos who made a profit within the solidarity group were forced to sacrifice their modest earnings in order to pay off debts incurred by their fellow members. Even though crop insurance had covered most of the losses from El Niño, it did not cover expenses associated with social benefits[16] or the personal loans that the companies had advanced to the farmers.

---

[16] These benefits, paid for in part by the farmer, include social security (mainly free medical care for the farmer and his family and a retirement pension through the Mexican Social Security Institute [IMSS]), crop insurance, and life insurance. ARIC is responsible for the administration of these services. Sugarcane is the only crop besides tobacco that provides automatic membership in the IMSS. The coffee sector lost access following the dismantling of the Mexican Coffee Institute (INMECAFÉ).

TABLE 2.3
AREA PLANTED IN TOBACCO AFTER THE DISMANTLING OF TABAMEX (HECTARES)

	1990–91	1991–92	1992–93	1993–94	1994–95	1995–96	1996–97	1997–98
Nayarit, Jalisco, Sinaloa	14,084	30,692	31,736	26,578	19,204	20,544	26,350	30,600
N. Veracruz (blond)	1,249	1,549	1,679	1,143	116	27	212	536
N. Veracruz (dark)	—	—	—	—	176	372	476	1,200
S. Veracruz[1] (dark)	700	755	852	978	1,300	1,500	2,950	2,912
Veracruz subtotal	1,949	2,304	2,531	2,121	1,592	1,899	3,638	4,648
Chiapas	1,957	1,886	1,420	1,112	666	926	2,423	1,994
Sonora	—	—	—	245	272	268	268	—
Total	17,990	34,882	35,687	30,056	21,734	23,637	32,679	37,242

Source: Developed from data collected by the author from ARIC in Nayarit and from tobacco companies.
[1] Data for Southern Veracruz are approximate.

At the season-end settlement, the number of farmers whose production was worth less than the value of the credit and technology package began to multiply as had never been seen previously. For the first time in the modern period of tobacco cultivation, there was widespread debt in both Nayarit and the Gulf zone. Thus tobacco went from being an excellent crop choice to being one of an array of poor choices. Many farmers continued to plant tobacco, but they reduced the area cultivated, hoping only to obtain the modest financial security that the credit and technology package provided by guaranteeing a flow of cash to be distributed as wages within the household.[17]

Farmers were also disgruntled about the new procedure for evaluating the quality of dried tobacco. During the last two years of TABAMEX, under pressure from the cigarette companies, a system involving four classifications representing different quality levels was instituted, as noted above. The number of classifications increased to seven in the 1993–1994 agricultural cycle and to twelve in 1994–1995 for all tobaccos except Virginia Hornos, for which there were eventually twenty classifications.[18] The difference in price between the highest and the lowest classification is substantial. For the farmers, this major change means that they have to be much more efficient in their application of the technological package in order to grow the more lucrative, high-quality tobaccos. Consequently, they have less opportunity to make a small profit on the side from the credit and technology package.

From the ARIC's perspective, the new procedures posed one of its biggest problems: how to resolve disagreements between buyers and sellers regarding the quality of the tobacco being offered for sale. Until the 1993–1994 agricultural cycle, the cigarette companies were in charge of the classification system but with the oversight of ARIC representatives. However, many complaints were registered about the behavior of the ARIC representatives, who were often accused of acting like company employees. At one point, it appeared that the matter would go to the Ministry of Agriculture for arbitration, but the SARH did not have staff with sufficient experience with tobaccos to intercede. Finally, beginning in 1994–1995, high-level officials from the companies and from ARIC were appointed to issue a judgment if

---

[17] Moreover, other crops do not include the type of worker benefits that come with tobacco cultivation.

[18] There are even more quality classifications (up to fifty) in other countries. The number varies according to the agronomic characteristics of the soil, the tobacco variety being cultivated, and the agreements with producers.

a disagreement persisted. In December 1996, when the fieldwork for this chapter was carried out, that was the system in force. Even though the number of complaints has declined in comparison to previous years as farmers have become accustomed to the new system and prices have risen somewhat following the devaluation of the Mexican peso at the end of 1994, concerns remain about finding a more objective way to evaluate the quality of processed tobacco.

In broad strokes, these are the principal problems that have affected farmers as a result of the deregulation of the tobacco sector. The tobacco growers of Nayarit used to be set apart by their relative prosperity in comparison with most tobacco smallholders elsewhere in Mexico; the contrast between Nayarit's tobacco farmers and the more typical campesinos who grow traditional crops like corn and beans is even more marked (see Giarracca 1983: 216–23). The income from tobacco grown on a parcel of land in Nayarit during a six- or seven-month cycle used to constitute the major share of support for the basic needs of a campesino household for an entire year. Following the privatization of TABAMEX, however, farmers in Nayarit have experienced a significant decline in their levels of well-being. And the campesino character of the production process has been reinforced, given that more manual labor is now provided by family members, and farmworkers are less and less frequently employed except during harvest and the curing of the tobacco leaf.[19]

Next we turn to an analysis of the role of ARIC in the reorganization of tobacco curing in Nayarit, a process where significant modernization has occurred even though the innovation affects only about 15 percent of the total area planted in tobacco in the state.

ARIC, Tadesa, and La Moderna: Decentralization and Modernization

Since the years of TERSA and during the TABAMEX period, farmers were accustomed to delivering recently harvested Virginia Hornos tobacco leaf to be dried in one of seven plants that together operated over 800 drying ovens in the municipality of Santiago Ixcuintla. After

---

[19] Campesinos whose family members are not available to help with the tobacco crop (because they have emigrated, for example) find it very difficult not to incur debt with the private companies. It is also important to note that tobacco fields traditionally were left fallow during the months between harvest and the next planting. During this period, campesinos often sought wage labor, even migrating temporarily to work in tobacco fields in the United States. Now, assuming that their parcels do not flood during the rainy season, the campesinos may also cultivate corn or some other crop that is covered by a small government subsidy through the PROCAMPO program.

the dismantling of TABAMEX, ARIC, the federal government, and the two companies that use Virginia Hornos tobacco—Cigatam and Cigarrera La Moderna—agreed that ARIC would temporarily manage these plants,[20] charging by the ton of tobacco to be cured. Meanwhile, both companies would build, on the farmers' own land, as many ovens as were needed. Thus the companies, rather than continuing to cure tobacco leaves in the large factories, opted for a decentralized system of small-scale ovens, an arrangement that is the norm in other tobacco-growing countries. This measure was designed to circumvent factory workers' unions and avoid other labor problems.[21] From the farmers' perspective, this reorganization meant that they would become the managers of tobacco-drying installations on a reduced scale, with the legal obligations this entailed. Having to cure the tobacco themselves was not an appealing option, but because the companies were offering few contracts and paying low prices for the other varieties produced in the region, many farmers had no choice but to accept the new arrangement.

Even though both companies agreed to decentralize production, each proposed its own reorganization plan. Tadesa, the contracting firm that is part of Cigatam, pursued a plan that required a much smaller investment. Since 1991 it has constructed individually owned ovens[22] by means of a financial program that discounts the capital invested from the season-end settlement. The payments of the invested capital are staggered over a period of ten years. This change does not affect the usual organization of the agricultural process. Production is still organized around solidarity groups, whose members cultivate an average of 20 hectares and organize their harvesting in stages (as used to be done under TABAMEX) in order to avoid delivering all their tobacco to the ovens at the same time. Another measure taken by Tadesa was to decentralize the tobacco seedbeds to the farmers' own parcels, a practice followed in most tobacco-producing

---

[20] In the original government plan, it was anticipated that the tobacco-drying factories would be turned over to ARIC, on the assumption that the campesino organization would take charge of them permanently. Ultimately, ARIC did not acquire them because they would be used only for three agricultural seasons and then discarded.

[21] A union affiliated with the "official" Confederation of Mexican Workers (CTM) held the collective contract with TABAMEX and had won comparatively high wages and benefits for its workers. When TABAMEX was liquidated, the old collective contract was terminated, but the union continued to operate in the tobacco-drying factories under the conditions established by Mexico's Federal Labor Law.

[22] These drying ovens, built in the traditional style and similar to those in the TABAMEX factories, are constructed of brick. On average, one oven is needed for every 5 hectares planted in tobacco (or four ovens for a solidarity group cultivating 20 hectares).

countries. According to a Tadesa engineer, the fact that the seedbeds are now the farmers' responsibility will motivate them to improve the quality of their plants (author interview with Engelberto Sánchez López, August 1994).

Under Tadesa's "Brazilian model," the tobacco company only provides the credit and technology package and, eventually, capital investment loans (for drying ovens and farm equipment, for example) but remains as detached as possible from day-to-day production tasks.[23] By contrast, Agroindustrias Moderna, the contracting firm under Cigarrera La Moderna, adopted (after a two-year delay) a model of organization based on the U.S.–Canadian large-scale and technified system. Under the system of participation associations, the company provides capital and technology, and the campesinos contribute their land and labor. In this case, farmers of the Virginia Hornos variety have to join their contiguous parcels of land into "agroindustrial modules" that measure 60 hectares on average. The operation of these modules requires both extensive investments in machinery, equipment, and state-of-the-art ovens imported from Canada[24] and the active participation of the company in the day-to-day management of the business. Regarding the seedbeds, Agroindustrias Moderna has maintained the old centralized system and has even invested in constructing greenhouses in Nayarit and Chiapas, where seedlings of selected tobacco varieties are grown.

The participation associations were initially established for ten years, at the end of which time the campesinos were to take over the infrastructure. But with the December 1994 peso devaluation, the period was extended by an additional three to six years, depending on the date at which each module had begun operation. The company employs a full-time manager (often a partner in the association) who, together with a supervisor,[25] plans out and assigns the tasks to be completed daily. The campesinos who are members of the association have priority in being hired, but outside farmworkers are also employed when needed. There are modules in which the number of associates is very small (one has 100 hectares and only two landowners

---

[23] The model takes its name from the system commonly found in Brazil, but with the difference that in Mexico the solidarity groups are heterogeneous, whereas in Brazil they are based on the family unit.

[24] One oven of the "bulk curing barn" type is needed for every 6 hectares of tobacco. These ovens do a better job of curing and use less labor and energy than do traditional ovens. Moreover, they can be transported to a new location if the association fails.

[25] Supervisors of the contracting companies oversee an average of 200 hectares each.

as members), but most consist of many ejidatarios, each of whom contributes 2 to 3 hectares. In the case of modules with smaller memberships, the company must rely on outside labor, but in the other modules, the members themselves can earn wages throughout most of the season and they have a right to voice their opinion in monthly assemblies in which the module's supervisor participates as the company representative.

Agroindustrias Moderna's project appears to be more successful than that of Tadesa. In the latter case, disgruntled farmers have simply abandoned their ovens, and since 1993–1994 Tadesa has had to implement a compensation system, called the "curing credit," to offset sinking profits and keep the campesinos from going broke. Agroindustrias Moderna's problems have not been as severe, and its project has been growing year by year. In 1993–1994, seven modules encompassing 475 hectares were in operation; by 1995–1996, there were seventeen modules, covering 1,168 hectares.[26] The two companies, taken together, cultivated a total of 2,812 hectares of oven-quality tobacco during the latter cycle. But this figure is still far from the average of 7,300 hectares that were under cultivation during the final two seasons when the tobacco-drying factories still operated— that is, between 1992 and 1994 (see note 14). This is evidence of the difficulty in pressing ahead too hard and fast with decentralization of the ovens.

Through the 1993–1994 season, the ARIC played the unfortunate role of managing the curing of tobacco belonging to Agroindustrias Moderna and Tadesa, a task that involved laying off nearly 3,000 part-time workers in January 1995 (*La Jornada*, January 15, 1995). These actions created tremendous ill-will in Santiago Ixcuintla, causing the takeover of oven installations and other public demonstrations and feeding a general discontent that would explode six months later.

The Resurgence of Grassroots Protest

Although it did not get worse, the overall economic picture for the tobacco sector showed no substantial improvement between 1992 and 1994. Most farmers complained that they were having to dig into their own pockets to cover the expenses incurred in the production process (author interviews). Although this claim is difficult to evalu-

---

[26] For more on the agro-industrial modules and on the restructuring of the tobacco sector, see Mackinlay n.d.

ate given that the companies insist the credit and technology package was sufficient to offset the costs of cultivating tobacco (but not for additional purposes, such as supplementing household income), farmers were finding it increasingly difficult to cover their daily basic consumption needs.

Moreover, the farmers' debts were growing. Despite a slowing in the rate of indebtedness, outstanding loans still represented an unresolved problem, and prospects for the season-end settlements were far from bright. On top of this, during 1994–1995, the area under cultivation in Nayarit alone dropped by more than 7,000 hectares compared to the previous year (see table 2.3). This decline was due to the negative outlook for the tobacco sector nationwide; the overvaluation of the peso had reduced the competitiveness of Mexican tobacco on the international market.

The December 1994 devaluation of the peso suddenly improved tobacco's prospects. At the end of the 1994–1995 season, the farmers' debt was less onerous and the settlements received were larger, even though the tobacco companies were the primary beneficiaries of the devaluation. The export companies did especially well, having settled on a price with ARIC in September 1994, before the devaluation; after the devaluation they were able to sell the processed tobacco at a very favorable exchange rate. This generated substantial discontent among the farmers who received settlements in May and June 1995. Under the leadership of Ramón López Tirado[27] and the influence of an important group of Barzonistas[28] that had formed in Santiago Ixcuintla, they resuscitated the FDT, the grassroots organization that had incited the protests in 1989 and 1990, when TABAMEX withdrew.

The rejuvenated FDT quickly incited an important mobilization in the tobacco-producing regions of Nayarit, which culminated in August 1995 with the takeover of the ARIC offices in Tepic, demonstrations in the center of the city, and a sit-in in front of Nayarit's state house, as well as the threat of a takeover of the local offices of the contracting companies. The principal demand was for compensation for the farmers in light of the extraordinary profits the companies presumably had made as a result of the peso devaluation. The

---

[27] From 1991 to 1994, while he was a federal deputy for the Party of the Democratic Revolution (PRD), López Tirado was out of the state most of the time. He returned to run unsuccessfully for state governor in 1993, on the Labor Party (PT) ticket.

[28] Barzonistas are members of a debtors' movement (El Barzón) that appeared during 1993. The movement consists primarily of small and midsize farmers in the ejidal and private sectors. Since its founding, the organization has spread throughout Mexico, including in urban areas.

state government responded rapidly. It jailed López Tirado on an outstanding arrest warrant, although the specific charges had nothing whatever to do with the tobacco issues, and it launched a smear campaign against him with the help of the Labor Party (PT) and the Party of the Democratic Revolution (PRD), parties with which López Tirado was on the outs. López Tirado was obliged to "retire" from politics, and the movement dissolved under the threat of government repression (author interviews).

Although it was quashed, the 1995 mobilization had an impact in the 1995–1996 season on the price of tobacco, which had not changed since 1990–1991. As a result of the devaluation, the price would have risen anyway, but because of the mobilization it probably rose more than it otherwise might have. Prices increased by about 30 percent in 1995–1996 and by 27 percent in 1996–1997 (see note 14). The area cultivated in tobacco did not increase during the first season, but it did in the second, due to the rising price for processed tobacco in the international market (see table 2.3).

ARIC's Role in the New Tobacco Agro-Industry

ARIC was able to resist the attacks from the FDT because the state government and the contracting companies continued to support it. But because of its role in the restructuring of the agro-industry in favor of Mexican and transnational corporations, it is highly unpopular among the campesinos. Nevertheless, ARIC is critically important to the state government because, as a pro–ruling party organization, it facilitates government control over tobacco growers. The government has had a strong influence over ARIC's administrative council, and the council's president (ARIC's top official) has close ties to the private companies. And on many occasions, ARIC, the state government, and the private companies have presented a united front against challenges that threaten the status quo.[29]

This is not to say that ARIC accepts unquestioningly whatever the government forces upon it, or that it does not have its own internal life. Like most CNC organizations, it is not noted for its democratic practices nor for the transparency of its financial dealings, but it has

---

[29] The state government of Nayarit, bastion of the CTM since the 1980s, is dominated by PRI hard-liners who act in an authoritarian manner to preserve their privileged status and the sinecures of Nayarit's power elite.

conducted internal elections with relative regularity.[30] Delegates from all regions of the state, although not seated at the negotiating table, participate in annual collective bargaining meetings; and they debate (and for the most part approve) proposals made by the administrative council. ARIC has its own agenda, which covers two principal issues. First, because they lived through the dismantling of TABAMEX, at which time ARIC was being considered as the potential coordinator of the credit and technology package, the organization's leaders still hope that ARIC will be involved in the future in the production process, to the benefit of its members. Second, after decades of state paternalism and corruption that produced attitudes and behaviors antithetical to sound business principles, ARIC's leaders recognize the need for technical training and a "new culture" among the farmers that will help to meet current demands for efficiency and productivity.[31]

There has been little headway made on either of these aims, however, starting with the fact that the first two leaders following the formation of ARIC very probably engaged in corrupt activities. Nevertheless, ARIC is affiliated with the London-based International Tobacco Growers' Association, and that connection helps ARIC stay informed about prices and international agricultural conditions. Since TABAMEX's privatization, ARIC has also won certain concessions relating to life insurance and crop insurance, and it has worked to improve the criteria used to classify tobacco, as well as developing a program of technical assistance for its associates that operates independently of those carried out by the private companies. ARIC also successfully opposed an increase in the number of quality categories in the 1996–1997 negotiations, and it intervenes in all important issues relating to the cultivation of tobacco, as well as being involved in the delivery of social services.

Because ARIC's leaders have relatively little negotiating experience, the organization is undergoing a learning process. It might be argued that it has not achieved very much—just the bare minimum to avoid an even greater isolation from its membership. However, it must also be stressed that it is not a company-controlled organization. Rather, it is a government-sponsored organization that was

---

[30] The last election for administrative council posts was scheduled for April 1996, but, at the request of the governor, it was postponed until September 9 to avoid coinciding with local elections. The state government in Nayarit has noticeably influenced the leadership succession within ARIC.

[31] Author interview (August 1994) with José Santos Navarro, president of the ARIC administrative council until September 1996.

controlled primarily by the federal government during the TABAMEX period and now is closer to the state government, even though the former still plays a role through the Ministry of Agriculture (SAGAR).[32]

From the point of view of the contracting companies, working with a unified organization representing all tobacco farmers has both advantages and disadvantages. On the one hand, the companies have far less maneuverability when negotiating with a union rather than the farmers themselves, either individually or in small groups. When dealing with an organization such as ARIC, the companies must make numerous concessions in order to preserve good relations with the union, and they must cultivate local leaders and political personalities.[33] They may also face pressure if the union becomes more demanding and combative. On the other hand, working with a unified organization with a large membership reduces transaction costs when negotiating prices for different tobacco varieties at the beginning of each season, the value of the credit and technology package, social welfare benefits, technology transfers, and implementation of measures related to the production process—as well as any and all questions or conflicts that might arise between the companies and the farmers.

Despite these considerations, the companies would probably prefer to act without the intermediation of a collective bargaining organization such as ARIC, as they advocated during the dismantling of TABAMEX. Nevertheless, given the economic, political, and social importance of tobacco production in that state, any attempt to alter the institutional framework for collective bargaining in Nayarit would surely have provoked strong objections from the federal and state governments. In other regions of Mexico where tobacco does not play such a strategic role, such as in Chiapas, private tobacco companies have been able to avoid working through a single organization. This was true, for example, of Agroindustrias Moderna, which managed to elude the mediating efforts of a campesino organization in Chiapas. In northern Veracruz, companies have opted to leave the

---

[32] Through the end of the Carlos Salinas de Gortari administration (1988–1994), Mexico's Ministry of Agriculture was known as the Ministry of Agriculture and Water Resources, or SARH. Under the following administration, that of Ernesto Zedillo Ponce de León (1994–2000), its name was changed to the Ministry of Agriculture, Livestock, and Rural Development, or SAGAR.

[33] José Santos Navarro, the second leader of ARIC who left office in September 1996, and Alfonso Langarica, an important statewide leader of the National Confederation of Rural Smallholders (CNPR), are both associated with Agroindustrias Moderna through their respective agro-industrial modules.

area or to reduce their presence when circumstances have been unfavorable. Thus the Gulf zone provides an interesting contrast to the case of Nayarit.

Restructuring Tobacco Production in the Gulf

While TABAMEX operated, the Gulf zone—Veracruz, Oaxaca, and Chiapas—had a disproportionate number of producers relative to its level of production. In the 1985–1986 season, this zone was home to 37 percent of the country's tobacco farmers, but it produced only 18 percent of Mexico's national output (TABAMEX 1989: 107, 112). Dark tobaccos, which were becoming harder to sell in the domestic and international markets, were grown primarily in northern Veracruz (Alamo, Platón Sánchez, and Papantla), central Veracruz near Córdoba, and around Tuxtepec and Zimatlán in Oaxaca and Zimojovel in Chiapas. TABAMEX heavily subsidized these regions, characterized by subsistence farmers cultivating tobacco on small plots and enjoying a standard of living considerably lower than that of their counterparts in Nayarit.[34] The Gulf's most commercially successful areas, albeit not at the level of the Nayarit–Jalisco region, were San Andrés Tuxtla in southern Veracruz, which grew cigar tobacco, and the Soconusco region in coastal Chiapas, where TABAMEX introduced the cultivation of blond tobacco.

During the 1980s, TABAMEX began reducing its financed area in the Gulf zone, especially in Veracruz and Oaxaca (see table 2.1). During 1989, as part of the first steps toward divestment, TABAMEX withdrew completely from Oaxaca. By the time the tobacco sector was deregulated, production outside the Nayarit–Jalisco zone was limited to the coast of Chiapas and northern and southern Veracruz. The next section focuses on these three areas.

Breakdown of Collective Bargaining: The Coast of Chiapas

Blond tobacco used in cigarettes is grown on the coast of Chiapas, even though climatic conditions (particularly the high humidity) are less favorable than those in Nayarit. Despite the region's limited production potential, it constitutes a reserve area for tobacco production

[34] For an analysis by region for the period when TABAMEX operated, see Giarracca 1983.

for the two large tobacco companies in case Nayarit suffers severe crop damage or some other problem.[35]

TABAMEX's administrative offices and warehouses were located in the town of Huixtla, Chiapas. Those facilities, along with transportation and irrigation infrastructure, were turned over to the Social Solidarity Society of Tobacco Producers of Chiapas (SSS), an association that had its roots in the State Union of Tobacco Producers (Unión Estatal de Productores de Tabaco) and was part of the CNC.

For the first two years following the dismantling of TABAMEX, the SSS operated in a fashion similar to ARIC in Nayarit, managing the relationship between producers and the tobacco companies. Nevertheless, the Chiapas tobacco farmers were disgruntled by the inequalities between the contracts negotiated for them and those negotiated for farmers in Nayarit. Among these inequalities were tobacco prices that were 15 to 20 percent lower than in Nayarit for the same tobacco varieties (the companies argued, as had TABAMEX, that this was due to discounts to cover the cost of transporting the crop from Chiapas to Nayarit's deveining plants). The amounts financed through the credit and technology package were smaller (supposedly because costs of production are lower in Chiapas), and the benefits package included only social security but no life or crop insurance.

In 1992, according to its then-president, Jorge López Vilchis, the SSS launched "an offensive, supported by the CNC, that won, for the first time in the history of Chiapas's tobacco cultivation, a purchase price that was the same as that offered in Nayarit" (López Vilchis 1993: 4). This accomplishment, in turn, sparked a campaign by Agroindustrias Moderna to convince the farmers to withhold their union dues and resign from the SSS, promising that the company would provide whatever was needed for production. Because of the mobilization over prices and other increasingly divisive issues, Agroindustrias Moderna ended its relationship with the SSS after the 1992–1993 season. This action, which left the SSS "decapitalized and bankrupt," was taken without regard for the agreement among the federal government, campesino organizations, and the tobacco companies to establish collective bargaining in each region along with a system for retaining dues from the season-end settlements so that the

---

[35] Near Tapachula, Grupo Pulsar (owner of Empresas La Moderna) has established the Centro Internacional de Investigación y Capacitación Agropecuaria, A.C., an important international agro-biotechnology research center. Here experiments are conducted to improve or develop seed stock, fresh produce for export, fruit trees, and tropical plants; and there is significant production of orchard and tobacco seedlings in greenhouses.

campesino organizations could repay the debt resulting from the acquisition of TABAMEX assets.[36]

After ending its relationship with the SSS, Agroindustrias Moderna chose to negotiate directly with tobacco growers from ejidos and municipalities that are at some distance from Huixtla. Thus, between 1990 and 1994, the SSS went from representing almost 890 farmers growing tobacco on 1,957 hectares to only 70 farmers working 152 hectares under contract with Tadesa.[37] The SSS now survives on its meager union dues and from rents collected on 58 irrigation rigs let out to tobacco farmers. During the two seasons following Agroindustrias Moderna's termination of its relationship with the SSS, the cultivated area under the company's control also declined noticeably. Rather than managing production through contracts, Agroindustrias Moderna primarily rented land directly, mostly from private owners of large fields, although it was also willing to rent smaller adjacent plots from ejidatarios in order to form large production areas. In contrast to the 2.2 hectares per producer that was the norm while the SSS operated, in Agroindustrias Moderna's fields during the 1995–1996 season, 720 hectares belonging to 19 producers were cultivated, at an average of 38 hectares per producer (author interview with Agroindustrias Moderna manager José González, February 1997).

After 1996, in the context of improved international tobacco prices, Agroindustrias Moderna launched a new program based on participation associations. Using the modular system, the company increased its involvement in the tobacco sector, going from thirteen modules encompassing a total of 720 hectares in 1995–1996 to twenty-four modules with a total of 1,914 hectares in 1996–1997. The plan was to continue enlarging so as to reach 2,400 hectares in the 1997–1998 season (author interview with José González). The modules in Chiapas that are dedicated to growing the oven-dried variety of tobacco are similar to those in Nayarit in terms of the infrastructure and contractual conditions, although contracts covering the production of Burley tobacco (which does not need ovens to be cured) are

---

[36] The agreement was made with Antonio Bassols (author interview, March 1997). However, no documents were signed that legally committed the tobacco companies to maintain it. The same thing occurred in other regions. The only signed documents are those that register the transfer (to the campesino organizations) and the sale (to the cigarette and export companies) of the parastatal's assets.

[37] Although it manages a considerably smaller area than Agroindustrias Moderna, Tadesa also reduced its cultivated area in Chiapas, from 436 hectares in 1990 to 152 in 1994. Tadesa's fields began to increase once again—to 206 hectares in 1995 and then to 507 hectares in 1996—when international tobacco prices started to rise (author interview with Miguel Osuna Gómez, Tadesa manager, February 1997).

made on a yearly basis. In this expansionary stage, Agroindustrias Moderna is no longer focusing on private property owners but is seeking small ejido parcels that can be joined together in fields averaging 60 hectares in size.[38]

In the case of Chiapas, negotiating with a single organization restricted Agroindustrias Moderna's maneuvering room, and the company opted to withdraw from the collective bargaining relationship in order to be freer to pursue its experiments and expansion. Where it was able to avoid the intermediation of campesino organizations, it has been able to select new partners and impose new rules. As a result, ejidatarios who had been SSS members, and whose standard of living is considerably lower than farmers in Nayarit, have now lost an important source of credit and income for their household economies. Because of their weak political influence, and because of the absence of binding contracts with the company, there was nothing they could do to prevent being dropped by Agroindustrias Moderna.

The Case of Veracruz

In Veracruz there was no unified state-level representation of tobacco producers during the TABAMEX period. In that state, many dispersed campesino organizations formed in the localities previously served by TABAMEX and asserted their right to the parastatal's assets. It is important to note that the market for dark tobacco, which predominates in Veracruz and is used mainly in cigar production, is very different from the market for blond cigarette tobacco. Cigar production and marketing is almost artisanal in character and involves many economic actors; in contrast, the cigarette industry is monopolized by a few huge national and transnational groups, which collude on many aspects of production and marketing.

WITHDRAWAL OF THE TOBACCO COMPANIES: NORTHERN VERACRUZ

In Alamo, in northern Veracruz, the assets of TABAMEX—administrative offices, transportation equipment, and warehouses—were divided between two organizations (an SSS affiliated with the CNC and

---

[38] In Chiapas, Grupo Pulsar has extended the use of the modular system to other crops (papaya, cantaloupe, watermelon, and bamboo, among others). According to Grupo Pulsar's president, Alfonso Romo, the modules in Chiapas, including those growing tobacco, cover about 4,500 hectares (*Expansión*, January 15, 1997).

an organization belonging to the National Movement of 400 Towns)[39] in proportion to the number of producers belonging to each. In Platón Sánchez as well, the assets were divided between two organizations, an ARIC and an SSS, both CNC affiliates. But in Papantla, the tobacco growers agreed to unite in a single organization, an SSS that is also an affiliate of the CNC.

During the first part of the 1990s, Agroindustrias Moderna and Tadesa dramatically reduced their involvement in the region from 1980s levels (see tables 2.2, 2.3). The tobacco companies were gradually withdrawing from the area even though they still needed some dark tobacco for certain brands and blends. But by the beginning of the 1995–1996 growing season, Agroindustrias Moderna had departed completely, and Tadesa maintained only a very reduced level of activity.

Without doing a full-scale analysis of the problematic of tobacco production in northern Veracruz, certain points bear mentioning:

- In this region, as in all of the Gulf zone, high humidity makes it difficult to control infestations of *moho azul*, a fungus that has become resistant to the chemical fungicides previously used to control it. This is not an insurmountable problem, but it makes tobacco cultivation more difficult.

- During the first part of the 1990s, citrus cultivation presented farmers with a viable alternative to tobacco cultivation.

- As in Nayarit, the tobacco farmers suffered a significant decline in their profits and were subjected to measures to improve productivity (reduced credit and technology packages, the implementation of quality classifications, and so forth).

- Problems arose between the tobacco companies and the farmers and their representative organizations, resulting in difficulties in implementing the new system of contract agriculture.

In fact, the farmers lost interest in tobacco cultivation because it demanded intense effort for little or no gain. Given that they needed the financing and social welfare benefits that came with the contracts, they did not refuse to sign up, but they also did not go out of their way to grow a crop that would meet quality standards. According to

---

[39] This semi-official union is headed by César del Angel, a longtime leader with close ties to the CNC and a critic of the Salinas administration's reforms to Article 27 of the Mexican Constitution.

Tadesa's manager in Papantla, the companies left because of low levels of productivity (aggravated by the *moho azul*) and because their withdrawal would not generate political or social unrest because farmers were slowly finding alternative crops to plant (author interview with Javier García Ramírez, May 1997). Nevertheless, the tobacco companies' departure brought a significant loss of income and employment to this rural area.

On the other hand, it should be noted that throughout the Gulf region, the rules governing contract agriculture have always been easily undermined for the simple reason that dark tobaccos can be sold clandestinely to other buyers, unlike the blond varieties, which are purchased solely by a handful of cigarette companies and exporters. Farmers in the Gulf were accustomed to earning additional income by selling part of the dark tobacco financed by Agroindustrias Moderna and Tadesa (and before them, by TABAMEX) to independent buyers who market it as cheap tobacco in nearby mountain communities or to representatives of small artisanal cigar factories. As demand for this kind of tobacco rose, so too did the amount of the diverted production.

A recent development in the tobacco sector is the impressive growth during the mid–1990s of cigar consumption in industrialized countries, perhaps in response to widespread anti-tobacco campaigns. As an example of what this change has meant for the tobacco sector, in 1997 several farmers working under contract with Tadesa to plant 135 hectares near Papantla opted to sell their crop to a buyer who offered them three times the price they would have received from Tadesa. The farmers then attempted to repay the cost of the credit and technology package they had received from Tadesa for that agricultural cycle. This, of course, was unacceptable to Tadesa, and the advanced money was deposited in an escrow account pending the outcome of a lawsuit to be filed against the farmers. Although the withdrawal of the tobacco companies from northern Veracruz occurred before the increase in cigar consumption was visible, the new situation will make the companies rethink the framework for contract agriculture, in case they decide someday to return to the area.[40]

The cigarette companies are being replaced by cigar companies such as Alfredo y Silvio Pérez Enterprises (ASP, Inc.), a Miami-based marketing company for dark tobaccos, which formed a partnership with ARIC Tabacalera and Agropecuaria de Platón Sánchez (an or-

---

[40] Tadesa increased somewhat its level of participation in Papantla and returned to Platón Sánchez in 1997. Alamo has no tobacco-growing activities.

ganization that previously worked with Agroindustrias Moderna) to cultivate 176 hectares during the 1994–1995 cycle, 372 in 1995–1996, and 476 in 1996–1997 (see the data for cigar tobaccos in northern Veracruz in table 2.3). As is the case with the Primitivo R. Valencia Ejido Union (UEPRV) in San Andrés Tuxtla in southern Veracruz, which will be discussed in the following section, contract agriculture continues but in a modified fashion in virtue of the greater demand that exists for dark tobacco.

CONTRACT AGRICULTURE AND LEASING: THE CASE OF SOUTHERN VERACRUZ

In San Andrés Tuxtla, unlike any other place in Mexico, TABAMEX was not the only actor buying and selling tobacco. Instead, it coexisted with companies belonging to longtime tobacco-farming families—Turrent, Carrión, Ortiz, and others—which mainly sold processed tobacco in the international market but also ran their own cigar factories. Before the arrival of the parastatal, these families grew tobacco on their own land and also rented ejidatarios' fields (despite legal prohibitions against this practice),[41] employing the ejidatarios as farmworkers. Contract agriculture as such did not really exist. By renting land to farm, the family-run companies did not delegate production responsibility, as happens under the credit-and-technology-package system. Rather, they took direct control of production in order to guarantee a high-quality tobacco leaf. This situation continued after the arrival of TABAMEX: the families remained active in tobacco although they cultivated less land because the parastatal had established contract agriculture on ejidal fields formerly rented out to the families.

During the TABAMEX period, financing for agricultural production did not come from the tobacco companies because these companies were not interested in the cigar business. However, the banking sector was very willing to provide loans given the fact that tobacco grown in San Andrés sold on the international market (Giarracca 1983: 164). The presence of TABAMEX in the area meant considerable social progress for the ejidatarios. They could take advantage of the new credit and technology packages, and their incomes rose substantially over earlier periods when the ejidatarios had rented out their fields and worked for the family-run companies. As in the other regions, siphoning off part of the credit and technology package was

---

[41] To circumvent this prohibition, the tobacco-farming families and ejidatarios would pretend that there was a credit-and-technology-package arrangement between them.

a common practice, but in San Andrés it was also possible to sell part of the tobacco crop financed by TABAMEX to the factories belonging to the family-run cigar companies. Thus, because the parastatal did not have a complete monopoly over tobacco purchasing, the cigar companies that were able to buy tobacco leaf illegally at bargain prices reaped substantial benefit.

The cigar companies did not participate in the divestment of TABAMEX. All of the assets—offices, warehouses, a laboratory, pickups, tractors, transport trucks, irrigation equipment, and 152 drying sheds, with a combined value of about U.S.$2 million—were turned over to the Primitivo R. Valencia Ejido Union.[42] From the outset, the UEPRV has enjoyed the support of Gustavo Carvajal Moreno, the last director general of TABAMEX and later a PRI senator from Veracruz. The UEPRV has also maintained a relationship with one of TABAMEX's principal foreign clients, ASP, Inc. in Miami, and it gets its financing directly from the banks (just as TABAMEX had) and from ASP itself.

After a difficult start in March 1990 followed by numerous ups and downs, the UEPRV has consolidated little by little. By 1995–1996 it was financing 213 producers, a figure that increased in 1996–1997 to 360 farmers cultivating 750 hectares. The UEPRV only processes dark tobacco and does not take part in cigar manufacturing. Approximately 82 percent of its output is sold abroad and 18 percent domestically. It employs about 600 workers in processing, and its members employ 1,500 workers, on average, in agricultural activities. By mid–1997 the UEPRV had twenty drying sheds under construction, financed by an ASP, Inc. investment of U.S.$950,000.[43]

The UEPRV continued the practice of contract agriculture but in a form that does not involve an unequal relationship with a private tobacco firm. The farmers are also the owners of the company and thus make a profit on top of the season-end settlement. Nevertheless, approximately 40 tons of tobacco were pilfered by union members in

---

[42] Another organization, the Enrique López Huitrón Ejido Union, was formed as a result of a disagreement with the UEPRV leaders' position on the TABAMEX assets. The founders of this new organization argued that it was not necessary to pay for the TABAMEX assets, because they belonged to the campesinos by right. They got bank financing to provide credit and technology packages to the membership in the 1990–1991 season, but the organization ceased operations before the end of the season and never returned the money lent to it by the bank. It appears that the most powerful of the local private companies—that of the Turrent family—was manipulating this organization with the aim of weakening the UEPRV.

[43] Transcript of a speech by Alain White Herrera, president of the administrative council of UEPRV, during a visit by President Ernesto Zedillo to Veracruz, May 1997.

1993, and this forced the union to work during 1994 to cover its losses.[44] Some of the steps that the UEPRV has taken to avoid inefficiencies and to raise productivity and quality are similar to those employed by the private tobacco companies. They include measures such as strictly managing the organization's resources and establishing three quality categories for the purchase of tobacco (an arrangement considerably more benevolent than the multiple-category system used by the tobacco companies). However, the most important measure is related to the sale price: at the end of the agricultural cycle, the farmer receives an initial payment for the tobacco based on a relatively low guaranteed price, but a final settlement is made later based on the amount that is actually received at the time of sale on the open market. By contrast, the tobacco company negotiators settle on a payment price before the agricultural season even starts, and it is based on very conservative estimates designed to guarantee high profits for the company.

As had been the case for TABAMEX, the UEPRV must coexist with the family-run companies, which by the beginning of 1997 consisted primarily of the Turrent and Ortiz families. The property and cigar factory belonging to the Carrión family was taken over by Agroindustrias Moderna, which had been operating in the area for two years in response to the growing international demand for dark tobacco and cigars (see table 2.3). The company Nueva Matacapan Tabacos, belonging to the Turrent family, has approximately 400 hectares and produces 60 percent of its raw material on its own lands and 40 percent on rented fields or fields financed through a credit and technology package.[45] This was the first time that the Turrent company had adopted the contract agriculture system, but it did so only for poorer quality tobaccos used to pack the cigars; and even in this case, it maintains careful control over the production process.[46] Whether on its own land or on rented fields, the company directly oversees the cultivation of the highest quality tobacco, whose leaves are used to wrap the cigar. In addition to these companies, there has been a proliferation of independent growers and small cigar factories in the region in response to rising international prices.

---

[44] Alain White Herrera admonished the producers in a general assembly regarding this loss, telling them that they "were stealing from themselves."

[45] Author interview with Alberto Turrent Cano, director general of Nueva Matacapan Tabacos, May 1997.

[46] Cigarette companies typically have supervisors who oversee an average of 200 hectares each, while in the case of Nueva Matacapan, supervisors are each responsible for no more than 80 hectares.

Agroindustrias Moderna, for its part, rented 220 hectares during the 1996–1997 season. And, as is its style, it has been making major investments in the area. To convince campesinos to rent out their plots, the company is offering them agricultural jobs at wages significantly higher than can be made working for other companies (including the UEPRV); these wages are in addition to the rents the farmers will collect on their land. Because it is a recent arrival in the area, Agroindustrias Moderna is still in an experimental phase. To make use of heavy machinery and economies of scale, it has rented contiguous small parcels of land in order to consolidate them into large fields, but it has yet to decide if it is going to operate by renting land or if it will propose a framework of participation associations, similar to the agro-industrial modules that it developed in Nayarit.

In conclusion, it should be emphasized that the UEPRV is a campesino organization that operates as a direct producer of cigar tobacco, managing almost 40 percent of all the area cultivated in tobacco in this part of Veracruz. It is the only campesino-run company in the ejidal sector to have become directly involved in tobacco production. ARIC Tabacalera and Agropecuaria de Platón Sánchez, in northern Veracruz, may follow in its steps if, in coming years, they manage to consolidate connections to international markets. The UEPRV is *not*, however, an umbrella organization advocating for the campesino tobacco producers of southern Veracruz as a bloc, a role that no organization has taken up as yet. Outside the UEPRV's sphere of influence, the private companies (Turrent, Ortiz, and Agroindustrias Moderna, principally) negotiate with campesinos individually or in small groups (very similar to the pattern in Chiapas) to establish the terms of the relationship, whether it be through land rental contracts, credit and technology packages, or possibly, in the near future, tobacco production associations. Considering the economic difficulties across all of Mexico's rural sector, the campesinos in this region often have no option but to accept unfavorable conditions when negotiating and signing such agreements.

Conclusion

Campesino organizations in the tobacco sector today play a role entirely unlike what had been envisioned for them in the initial proposal for the dismantling of TABAMEX. This proposal was aimed at limiting the monopolistic powers of the huge Mexican conglomerates and transnational companies that produce cigarettes and export processed tobacco.[47] The reorganization of the tobacco sector has resulted instead in overprotection of private-sector interests, in detriment to the tobacco farmers, who have suffered a serious decline in their standard of living.

When comparing today's situation to the period when TABAMEX operated, one notes that the parastatal, acting as an intermediary between the growers and the tobacco companies, upstaged the campesino organizations in decision making. Under today's arrangements in Nayarit, a direct relationship exists between the farmers' organizations and the contracting companies, without the participation of federal or state government agencies. This institutional arrangement differs from what existed during the days when TERSA operated (that is, pre–1972). At that time negotiations took place only with individual farmers or small groups of farmers, something that occurs today in Chiapas and Veracruz, cases where the similarities to that earlier period are easily visible.

A single, relatively powerful collective-bargaining organization was preserved in Nayarit, something that did not happen in the other tobacco-growing regions of Mexico. Although it is possible that this campesino organization in Nayarit may some day assume a direct role in the production process, neither this possibility nor the delivery of technical assistance and training can constitute the organization's primary concern. Involvement in these activities would represent a duplication of effort with the contracting companies. The most important and beneficial role that the organization could assume would be to provide an adequate level of mediation in negotiations over the many dimensions of the company-producer relationship, such as the price of processed tobacco (which includes quality classifications), the credit and technology package, crop insurance, and so on. Among other crucial issues, regulation is needed regarding the terms of the contracts offered to producers by Tadesa, with its decen-

---

[47] After the research for this chapter was completed in mid–1997, a major change of ownership occurred: all of Empresas La Moderna's tobacco business, including the cigarette company (Cigarrera La Moderna) and the contracting company (Agroindustrias Moderna) was sold by Grupo Pulsar to its previous owner and the second largest tobacco transnational in the world, British American Tobacco, for approximately U.S.$1.7 billion. This transaction was almost simultaneous with the takeover of Cigatam-Tadesa by Philip Morris, the world's leading cigarette company (Massieu 1998: 10). The transnationals' new expansionary trend in developing countries is a response to the difficulties these companies are encountering in industrialized countries, especially the United States, as a result of anti-tobacco campaigns.

tralized model, and Agroindustrias Moderna, with its agro-industrial modules.

The example of the UEPRV in southern Veracruz with regard to the criteria for pricing cigar tobaccos suggests that options exist for negotiating the price of cigarette tobacco as well. However, the lack of an organization to represent the campesinos who are not members of the UEPRV poses a problem.[48] Such an organization would be extremely valuable in this region, where rising international prices for dark tobaccos have spurred the appearance of multiple types of contracts and agreements that apply variously to wage and labor conditions, land rental, credit and technology packages, and probably, in the future, agro-industrial modules.

In Nayarit, regardless of the control exercised by private companies in all phases of production, if an organization were oriented less toward the preservation of the status quo (as is the case with ARIC) and more toward advocating for its members' interests, the tobacco farmers would have a better chance of achieving more satisfactory working conditions and earnings than they would without any organization. The withdrawal of the tobacco companies from northern Veracruz and the fragmentation of negotiations between producers and the companies in coastal Chiapas and southern Veracruz typify the difficulties that the absence of unified organizations creates for the producers. In those circumstances, private companies act virtually without limitation and can impose terms that are highly beneficial to themselves.

References

Bonfil, Alfredo V. 1986. "Reunión nacional sobre la producción, comercialización e industrialización de tabaco." In *Origen de una empresa pública. El caso de Tabacos Mexicanos*, edited by Antonio Chumacero. Nayarit: Universidad Autónoma de Nayarit.

Castellón Fonseca, Francisco Javier. 1992. "Tabaco y modernización en Nayarit (1930–1990)." In *Memoria del 75 aniversario del estado de Nayarit, 1917–1992*. Nayarit: Gobierno del Estado.

Chumacero, Antonio, ed. 1986. *Origen de una empresa pública. El caso de Tabacos Mexicanos*. Nayarit: Universidad Autónoma de Nayarit.

De la Fuente, Juan, and Horacio Mackinlay. 1994. "El movimiento campesino y las políticas de concertación y desincorporación de las empresas paraestatales rurales." In *Campo y ciudad en una era de transición*, edited by

---

[48] As noted above, tobacco growers on 60 percent of the total area planted in tobacco in southern Veracruz are not covered by the UEPRV.

Mario Bassols. Mexico City: Department of Sociology, Universidad Autónoma Metropolitana–Iztapalapa.

Giarracca, Norma. 1983. "La subordinación del campesinado a los complejos agroindustriales. El tabaco en México." Master's thesis, Universidad Nacional Autónoma de México.

González Castañeda, Héctor. 1995. "El tabaco: la mayor derrama económica para Nayarit," *Unir, Revista Trimestral de Vinculación de la Universidad Autónoma de Nayarit* 3 (January–March): 20–30.

Jáuregui, Jesús, et al. 1980. *Tabamex: un caso de integración vertical de la agricultura.* Mexico City: CIDER/Nueva Imagen.

La Moderna. 1996. "From Seed to Market: Empresas La Moderna's Agrobiotechnology Integration." Report NI-596-118. Cambridge, Mass.: Harvard Business School.

López Vilchis, Jorge. 1993. "Intervención en la reunión del Consejo de la Unión Nacional de Productores de Tabaco," *Minuta.* Mexico City, August 5.

Mackinlay, Horacio. 1996. "La CNC y el Nuevo Movimiento Campesino." In *Neoliberalismo y reorganización social en el campo mexicano,* edited by Hubert C. de Grammont. Mexico City: Plaza y Valdés.

————. n.d. "Nuevas tendencias de la agricultura de contrato: los productores de tabaco en Nayarit después de la privatización de Tabamex (1990–1997)." In *Empresas, restructuración productiva y empleo en la agricultura mexicana,* edited by Hubert C. de Grammont. Mexico City: Instituto de Investigaciones Sociales, Universidad Nacional Autónoma de México/Plaza y Valdés. Forthcoming.

Malo Juvera Castañeda, Karla. 1996. "La industria cigarrera en México." Bachelor's thesis, Instituto Tecnológico Autónomo de México.

Massieu, Yolanda. 1998. "ELM: A New Global Player in the Vegetable Market," *Biotechnology and Development Monitor* [University of Amsterdam] 34 (March).

Saldívar Von Wuthenau, Juan. 1991. "La desincorporación de empresas estatales en México: el caso de Tabamex." Bachelor's thesis, Instituto Tecnológico Autónomo de México.

TABAMEX (Tabacos Mexicanos, S.A. de C.V.). 1989. *Atlas del tabaco en México.* Mexico City: TABAMEX/Instituto Nacional de Estadística, Geografía e Informática.

Teubal, Miguel, et al. 1982. *El desarrollo agroindustrial y los sistemas no alimentarios: tabaco.* Documentos Técnicos para el Desarrollo Agroindustrial. Mexico City: Secretaría de Agricultura y Recursos Hidráulicos.

Valtierra Pacheco, Esteban. 1984. "La evolución del complejo sectorial tabacalero (1765–1982)." Bachelor's thesis, Universidad Autónoma Chapingo.

3

Reconstructing Institutions for Market Governance: Participatory Policy Regimes in Mexico's Coffee Sector

Richard Snyder

In 1989, after two decades of extensive intervention in production and marketing of coffee, the Mexican Coffee Institute (INMECAFÉ) began to withdraw.[1] The withdrawal of this state-owned enterprise was part of a larger set of neoliberal reforms expected to stimulate economic growth by reducing government intervention in the economy and increasing the role of market forces. INMECAFÉ's dismantling meant elimination of production supports, regulated prices, and government control of marketing channels for Mexico's 300,000 small coffee producers.[2] These reforms were intended to replace govern-

Research for this chapter was supported by a National Science Foundation Graduate Fellowship, a Fulbright Fellowship from the Institute for International Education, and grants from the Institute for the Study of World Politics and the Ejido Reform Research Project of the Center for U.S.–Mexican Studies at the University of California, San Diego. Portions of the chapter were written while the author was a Visiting Research Fellow at the Center for U.S.–Mexican Studies. He wishes to acknowledge the generous help of the many campesinos, rural development workers, and state and federal government officials in Mexico who shared their experiences and trusted his pledge of confidentiality. For helpful comments and suggestions on this material, the author thanks Jonathan Fox, Judy Harper, and Luis Hernández.

[1] Between 1970 and 1989, coffee accounted for an average of 5.1 percent of the total value of Mexico's exports and 34 percent of the total value of agricultural exports. Approximately three million Mexicans derive some part of their income from the coffee sector (Díaz Cárdenas et al. 1991: 67).

[2] Small producers are defined as those with less than 20 hectares (roughly 50 acres) of land.

ment intervention with unfettered market forces, reorienting coffee producers toward free market signals and away from government regulatory agencies.

But the withdrawal of INMECAFÉ did not have the effects envisioned by the architects of Mexico's neoliberal reforms. In the wake of INMECAFÉ's exit, Mexico's coffee producers did not find themselves face to face with free markets. Instead, they confronted a new, and in many ways more complex, regulatory environment composed of multiple actors that had entered the breach opened by the withdrawal of the old state-owned enterprise. These actors—other federal agencies, the governments of Mexico's coffee-producing states, and grassroots producer organizations—competed to control the policy areas vacated by INMECAFÉ. Most notably, INMECAFÉ's dismantling created new opportunities for state governments and regional producer organizations[3] to engage in market regulation and sectoral policy making, triggering a decentering of policy arenas from Mexico City to the capitals of the coffee-producing states.

Rather than leading to unregulated markets, then, neoliberal reforms in Mexico's coffee sector unleashed a complex process of shifting policy arenas and institution building that resulted in a variety of new, regulated market structures. This "reregulation" process was driven largely by political struggles between state governments and producer organizations to control the emerging policy arenas and define how coffee markets would be reorganized after INMECAFÉ's exit (see Snyder 1999a).

These contests between state governments and producer organizations resulted in new subnational institutions for sectoral policy making, or policy regimes, across Mexico's coffee-producing states. In some states (Puebla and Guerrero, for example), the new policy regimes reproduced long-standing patterns of top-down, exclusionary policy making and served mainly as conduits through which the ruling Institutional Revolutionary Party (PRI) sought to secure political support in the coffee sector. In other states, most notably Oaxaca, government agencies and producer organizations worked together to build institutions that combined producer participation in policy making with a public-sector role focused on creating comparative market advantage. In addition to meeting producers' demands for a voice in the policy-making process, these participatory policy regimes helped coffee producers improve their welfare and market competitiveness.

---

[3] The concept of "region" is used in this study to refer to subnational territorial units, which, in the Mexican context, often encompass several municipalities but usually do not extend to an entire state.

This chapter analyzes the construction and performance of the participatory policy regime that emerged in Oaxaca after INMECAFÉ's dismantling,[4] and argues that this policy regime resulted from the intersection of a neocorporatist project intended to rejuvenate officially controlled channels of campesino interest representation with a powerful, autonomous producer movement that mobilized against that project. Subnational authoritarian elites, through their efforts to strengthen corporatist frameworks of controlled interest mediation, unintentionally provided incentives and institutional raw materials that helped a grassroots producer movement construct a participatory policy regime.

The first section of the chapter focuses on the populist policies pursued by the state government of Oaxaca in the late 1980s, showing how that government in many ways reproduced at the subnational level the statist economic policies that had characterized the national level in Mexico during the 1970s.[5] The government of Oaxaca sought to fill policy vacuums created by the federal government's neoliberal economic reforms with new regulatory institutions and frameworks of controlled interest group representation. In its focus on constructing new institutions, the populist government of Oaxaca supplied key building blocks that grassroots coffee producer organizations used to create a participatory policy regime.

The next section explores the dramatic changes in the organizational profile of Oaxaca's coffee sector during the 1980s, focusing on the emergence of independent producer organizations autonomous from government-controlled corporatist channels. These independent groups formed the backbone of a new, statewide coffee producers' confederation that organized against the government of Oaxaca's neocorporatist project. The discussion reveals how this confederation forged a participatory policy regime by successfully challenging the state government's efforts to impose a top-down framework on the coffee sector when INMECAFÉ withdrew.

The following section focuses on the dynamics of the participatory policy regime, analyzing the remarkable successes of Oaxaca's State Coffee Council. It highlights how collaboration between producer organizations and state government through the State Coffee Council redefined the roles of grassroots organizations and government in ways that helped improve the welfare of small coffee producers.

The conclusion considers the lessons the case of Oaxaca offers about how to achieve participatory institutions for market governance. Politicians with state-building proclivities and powerful grass-

---

[4] On the varied types of policy regimes that emerged in Mexico's other major coffee producing states after INMECAFÉ's dismantling, see Snyder 1999a, n.d.

[5] On subnational political regimes in Mexico, see Fox 1996; Snyder 1999b; Rubin 1996.

roots organizations capable of managing key economic activities both seem core ingredients of participatory policy regimes.

Neoliberal Center, Populist Periphery: The Populist Government in Oaxaca

Heladio Ramírez López was a surprising choice as the PRI's candidate in Oaxaca's gubernatorial election of 1986. Ramírez's political career had taken off in the early 1970s with the support of close advisers to President Luis Echeverría (1970–1976), and his political vision and policy preferences had been forged in the mold of the statist-populist policies dominant at that time. His policy orientations were strongly at odds with the neoliberal, technocratic approach characterizing Miguel de la Madrid's (1982–1988) presidency. This technocratic orientation was reflected in de la Madrid's marked preference for gubernatorial candidates with strong administrative credentials.[6] Ramírez, by contrast, was a career politician with modest administrative experience.

In addition to being out of step with prevailing national policy currents, Ramírez faced strong opposition from Oaxaca's private-sector elite. Local elites blamed the populist policies of Echeverría for the intense social unrest that had rocked Oaxaca in the 1970s, resulting in removal of a conservative, pro-business governor.[7] They viewed Ramírez's nomination as the harbinger of another round of social instability and government confrontation with the private sector. Oaxaca's most important newspapers vocally expressed the local elites' fears, greeting the news of Ramírez's nomination with headlines proclaiming a "black night for Oaxaca" and denouncing the candidate as a "delirious leftist" (*Noticias*, April 1–2, 1986).

Ramírez's choice of advisers reflected his ideological formation. His team included several professors from the National Autonomous University of Mexico's (UNAM) Department of Economics, which had a strong structuralist, statist orientation.[8] Their policy perspectives were a far cry from those of the typically foreign-trained, neo-

---

[6] De la Madrid's preference for technocrats as governors is illustrated by his choice of gubernatorial candidates such as the following: Rodolfo Félix Valdés in Sonora; ex-secretary of energy, mines, and parastatal industry Francisco Labastida Ochoa in Sinaloa; and, in the state of Michoacán, ex-secretary of agrarian reform José Luis Martínez Villicaña (Yescas Martínez 1991: 29).

[7] On the fall of Governor Manuel Zárate Aquino (1974–1977), see Martínez Vásquez 1990: chap. 4.

[8] Examples include Armando Labra, who advised the governor on social policy, and David Colmenares Páramo, who served as secretary of the treasury.

liberal economists who advised the president. As one of Ramírez's advisers put it, "We were taboo for the neoliberals. They thought we were from a premodern epoch" (author interview, June 1995).

Besides academics who rejected the prevailing neoliberal orthodoxy, Ramírez's circle of advisers also included prominent individuals who had held high-level federal government posts during Echeverría's administration. Fausto Cantú Peña, whom Ramírez invited to supervise policy for the coffee sector, had served as INMECAFÉ's director under Echeverría. Augusto Gómez Villanueva, who advised Ramírez on rural policy issues, had directed the federal Department of Agrarian Affairs and Colonization during Echeverría's administration. They brought to Ramírez's government considerable hands-on experience administering populist policies.

These advisers' vision of the public sector's appropriate role was articulated by the doctrine of social liberalism and the related concept of "social rule of law" (*estado social de derecho*).[9] This doctrine justified government regulation to promote social and economic welfare. As stated in the official document summarizing the "legal framework" for Ramírez's administration, the doctrine of social rule of law sought to "overcome the limitations of classical, individualistic liberalism, which was characterized by state abstention, by means of dynamic state activity that ... promotes social justice and welfare." The document criticized perspectives that viewed the state's role as limited to contract enforcement and protection of individual rights, because such perspectives were "imbued with a liberal, individualistic philosophy that paralyzes [the state's] activity and minimizes its role" (Gobierno 1992a: 18). Another official document described Ramírez's government as "permeated by the ideology of social liberalism" and characterized by an ongoing quest for "increasing state intervention" in order to "coordinate and harmonize [Oaxaca's] diverse interest groups" and "redistribute goods and services according to the necessities of each [of Oaxaca's] regions" (Gobierno 1992b: 249).

Their efforts to reform the constitution of Oaxaca in order to codify government responsibility for economic management and development indicate that Ramírez and his advisers took this rhetoric seriously. The reform of Article 20 of the state constitution affirmed the public sector's role as "rector" of economic development and granted it power to take measures necessary to promote Oaxaca's economic and social development. This constitutional reform delegated broad

---

[9] The concept of "social liberalism" was in vogue at the national level after President Salinas introduced it in 1989 during his second State of the Nation address. See Cornelius, Craig, and Fox 1994: 4, n. 1. See Villarreal 1993 for a fuller elaboration. The concept of social rule of law, however, seems to have been developed by Ramírez's team.

responsibilities to the public sector, stipulating that "the state will plan, implement, coordinate, and orient local economic activity and carry out the regulation and promotion of those activities corresponding to the public interest" (Gobierno 1992b: 45–46).

In addition to the State Coffee Council, which is analyzed below, new government institutions for economic management created during Ramírez's tenure included a parastatal to coordinate highway and airport infrastructure construction (Caminos y Aeropistas de Oaxaca), as well as an agency to supervise the lumber sector (Consejo Forestal y de la Fauna Silvestre del Estado de Oaxaca). Although the total number of such instances of state building was small (four or five), the surprising fact is that *any* new agencies for government economic intervention were created, given increasing national-level efforts during this period to reduce the public sector's role and dismantle government institutions.

Neocorporatist Coalition Building

The composition of Ramírez's internal support coalition is suggested by the response from a prominent member of Oaxaca's private-sector elite when asked to characterize his administration: "[Ramírez] governed for the poor and marginalized the rich" (author interview, June 1995). As noted above, Ramírez's relations with Oaxaca's private sector were strained even before he entered office. Rather than accommodate the local elite, he sought to construct a support coalition rooted in Oaxaca's social sector.

The principal tools Ramírez used to forge and sustain this coalition were the PRI's official corporatist organizations: the National Peasants' Confederation (CNC), within which he had held top national leadership positions, and the Confederation of Mexican Workers (CTM). These coalition-building tools had been blunted, however: internal inertia and corruption, combined with external competition from new, independent organizations that had proliferated across Oaxaca since the early 1970s, had weakened the traditional monopoly control of official corporatist unions. Ramírez sought to rejuvenate these declining corporatist mechanisms of controlled interest group representation, especially the CNC.

Ramírez's government focused on promoting peasant unions, a task the governor had mastered during his tenure as the CNC's secretary of union affairs in the early 1980s. Oaxaca experienced a veritable explosion of official rural organizations. The overall organizational scheme was structured around branches of production and based on a three-tiered hierarchy: first-level organizations, such as ejidos and agrarian communities, were incorporated into second-level Unions of Ejidos (UEs); Unions of Ejidos were grouped into third-level, statewide Rural Collective Interest Associations (ARICs) (Gobierno 1992b: 55–59). ARICs performed a dual function, serving both as collective marketing boards and as sectoral peak organizations that monopolized interest intermediation for each agricultural production branch. Between 1986 and 1992, nine ARICs were created, and the total number of Unions of Ejidos increased tenfold, from nine to ninety.[10]

This organizing campaign, dubbed "the agricultural revolution through peasant organization," was touted by Ramírez's government as a rural development strategy that would yield substantial increases in agricultural productivity (Gobierno 1992b: 49). Not surprisingly, given Ramírez's political formation, this strategy of promoting second- and third-level organizations around production branches had been introduced in the mid–1970s during Echeverría's presidency (Fox and Gordillo 1989: 142–43). Despite the colorful rhetoric of promoting economic development that surrounded the government of Oaxaca's rural organizing campaign,[11] this project, like Echeverría's before it, was a top-down effort to revitalize corporatist mechanisms of state-controlled interest representation.

For example, Ramírez's government repeated an earlier practice established during Echeverría's administration of compulsory incorporation of rural communities into the new second- and third-level organizations. The Unions of Ejidos and ARICs in Oaxaca fostered many of the same abuses of power that had characterized the earlier, Echeverría-era projects. These new organizations were usually characterized by mismanagement of resources—and often by outright fraud and corruption. According to one federal government official who worked in Oaxaca during Ramírez's administration, many of the Unions of Ejidos were literally created overnight and served mainly as "legal shells" to secure funds for corrupt CNC leaders. From his frequent dealings with the coffee-sector ARIC, he concluded that its leadership's main objective was "to steal money" by obtaining fraudulent bank loans (author interview, December 1995).

In another revival of a pernicious practice from the Echeverría period, the National Rural Credit Bank (BANRURAL) played an active role through its local subsidiary (BANCRI S.A. de C.V.) promoting ARICs because it could unload huge loans easily by concentrating producers into large-scale agro-industrial and marketing projects. Such over-

---

[10] There had been no ARICs in Oaxaca previously. See Gobierno 1992b: 56.

[11] An example is Ramírez's proclamation that "Organization makes possible the miracle of transforming the weak into the strong, and the campesinos can achieve what they never could have individually" (Gobierno 1989a: 26).

sized loans also helped conceal the corruption of BANRURAL and ARIC officials.

These new state-sponsored organizations did not merely line the pockets of corrupt officials, however. They also served as tools for attempting to block expansion of producer organizations not affiliated with the PRI. When these independent organizations sought to join together to form their own Unions of Ejidos, in order to take advantage of special financing opportunities available to such entities, they often found they had been preempted by a CNC–affiliated union. For example, the independent Union of Indigenous Communities of the Northern Isthmus (UCIZONI) discovered that it could not form its own Union of Ejidos, because many of the ejidos to which its members belonged had already been incorporated into a CNC union (Aranda Bezaury 1992: 91). An independent group of INMECAFÉ's Economic Units for Production and Marketing (UEPCs)[12] in the Mazateca region encountered a similar obstacle. When they tried to break free from the official "Uni-Nuu" cooperative (a CNC–affiliated organization that formed the backbone of the coffee sector ARIC), the UEPCs were denied permission to form their own Union of Ejidos by the federal delegate of the Ministry of Agrarian Reform (author interview, December 1994).

In sum, despite rhetorical claims of igniting an "agricultural revolution," Ramírez's organizing campaign was more an effort to reassert state control over rural interest group representation in the context of a growing threat from independent producer organizations. The campaign's success in this respect was limited, especially in the coffee sector, where independent organizations expanded considerably during Ramírez's tenure. In the end, perhaps the campaign's most concrete achievement was to create fresh opportunities for illicit enrichment by CNC and BANRURAL officials.

Given his government's overall focus on reviving mechanisms of controlled rural interest representation, it is not surprising that Ramírez responded to INMECAFÉ's withdrawal by launching a neo-corporatist reregulation project to occupy the domains of policy making and interest mediation abandoned by the federal agency. As illustrated by the rural organizing campaign, Ramírez's populist government sought to leave no political space unfilled. This imperative was especially strong in the coffee sector, because coffee was Oaxaca's most important agricultural activity, making a crucial contribution to the livelihoods of approximately 300,000 of the state's

---

[12] The UEPCs were collectivities of small producers that managed distribution and recuperation of credits and other inputs from INMECAFÉ. They formed the backbone of the parastatal's organizational infrastructure.

three million residents, and because independent grassroots organizations had made their greatest advances in this sector.

Hence, for Ramírez the challenge posed by INMECAFÉ's withdrawal was clear: build a new set of institutions under state government control to encapsulate small coffee producers, thereby stemming the spread of independent organizations. For this task, Fausto Cantú Peña, the architect of national coffee-sector policy under Ramírez's political mentor, President Echeverría, was the natural choice.

Remaking Neocorporatism from Below

When Cantú arrived in Oaxaca in late 1988, the vast majority of Oaxaca's small coffee-producers were affiliated with the CNC.[13] Although several autonomous producer organizations had formed outside the CNC's ranks, they were dispersed geographically and had established minimal linkages among themselves. Taken together, these independent organizations numbered at most 5,000 producers, less than 10 percent of the total number of producers in Oaxaca. From Cantú's perspective, Oaxaca must have seemed a propitious context for his neocorporatist project to exclude independent organizations and limit representation of small producers to official, CNC–affiliated groups.

Within just two years, however, the organizational profile of Oaxaca's coffee sector would be transformed dramatically, making Cantú's exclusionary project unfeasible. The independent producer organizations joined together to form a new, statewide coordinating network (*coordinadora*) that integrated 20,000, or almost 40 percent, of Oaxaca's 55,000 small coffee producers (Moguel and Aranda 1992: 187). This new organization—the Statewide Coordinating Network of Coffee Producers of Oaxaca (CEPCO)—quickly became the state's most powerful producer organization in terms of both size and mobilizational capacity. CEPCO's most notable early accomplishment was to challenge successfully the state government's neocorporatist project, forcing Cantú's ouster and transforming Oaxaca's emerging, post–INMECAFÉ policy regime from an exclusionary to a participatory one.

How can we explain the sudden formation of an independent movement with such a broad base of support? The movement's rapid emergence is especially puzzling because it occurred in the context of a government that, as we have seen, actively pursued a rural organiz-

---

[13] In most cases this affiliation was automatic by virtue of the producers' membership in INMECAFÉ's UEPCs, which entailed obligatory CNC membership.

ing campaign intended to prevent the spread of autonomous organizations. The material below suggests the following explanation for CEPCO's rapid formation. First, preexisting independent organizations had crucial mobilizational experience that enabled them to serve as "organizational pillars," which helped accelerate the construction of a new, statewide confederation. When these organizations joined to form CEPCO, they received pivotal support from allies within federal government agencies. In several instances, INMECAFÉ's field staff helped recruit into CEPCO newly available producers let loose by the dismantling of the parastatal's network of UEPCs. The facilitating role played by INMECAFÉ workers and CEPCO's strategy of actively recruiting UEPC members both help explain the dramatic expansion of the new organization's ranks. Furthermore, mid- and upper-level officials with federal social development agencies (especially the National Solidarity Program, or PRONASOL) provided important financial support to CEPCO, which helped the fledgling organization consolidate.[14]

Finally, the state government's neocorporatist project itself contributed to CEPCO's birth by providing new incentives for the dispersed independent organizations to join forces and mobilize to gain inclusion within the emerging policy regime. As one of CEPCO's leaders evocatively put it, Cantú's project was the unintended "detonator" for a wave of intense counter-mobilization that shattered the CNC's hegemony in Oaxaca's coffee sector.

CEPCO's engaged productivist strategy—which focused on challenging and seeking to modify the state government's initiative for the coffee sector, while avoiding affiliations with a political opposition party—also contributed significantly to the formation of Oaxaca's participatory policy regime. On the one hand, rather than pursuing a disengaged productivist strategy that ignored the governor's reregulation project and focused instead on autonomous economic development initiatives, CEPCO contested the project, demanding inclusion in the policy regime. On the other hand, CEPCO challenged the state government's reregulation project in nonpartisan terms, voicing opposition through interest group rather than electoral politics.[15]

This nonpartisan strategy combined with CEPCO's numerical strength to convince a reluctant Governor Ramírez to accept the independent organizations as legitimate actors in the post–INMECAFÉ policy arena. The fact that CEPCO had not allied with political op-

---

[14] CEPCO's formation exemplifies what Fox (1996) calls the "state-society convergence" pathway for accumulating social capital.

[15] On the alternative strategies pursued by coffee producer organizations in Mexico's other states, see Snyder 1999a, n.d.

position parties made it easier for the governor to acquiesce to the organization's demands for inclusion. And the very real threat that CEPCO might renounce its productivist position and affiliate with an opposition party if it were not included significantly raised the costs to Ramírez of inflexibility. As one participant commented, Ramírez recognized it was preferable to have CEPCO inside the coffee-sector policy regime where he could potentially control it, rather than "constantly mobilizing and making noise on the outside" (author interview, December 1995).

Organizational Pillars: The Independent Producer Organizations

In the late 1970s and early 1980s, a number of independent, small coffee-producer organizations formed across Oaxaca. As noted above, until 1989 these organizations were dispersed and made few efforts to coordinate their activities. This dispersion was due in part to Oaxaca's rugged, mountainous terrain, which posed natural barriers to interregional organizing. These barriers were reinforced by ethnic divisions: Oaxaca's population is divided into seventeen ethnic groups with distinctive languages and customs.[16] In 1988 the most important independent coffee-producer organizations were spread across four distinct regions populated by at least seven ethnic groups.[17]

In addition to these geographical and cultural barriers, the diverse developmental trajectories of the organizations further impeded interaction and coordination among them. Most had formed around distinct local issues not directly related to coffee production (such as improving access to food or securing better rural roads), gradually moving into coffee production and marketing. For example, the Union of Indigenous Communities "One Hundred Years of Solitude"(UCI "Cien Años"), which represented approximately five hundred producers from the coastal region, had formed in the early 1980s as an organization of Community Food Councils.[18] UCI "Cien Años" expanded into coffee production in the mid–1980s (author interviews, December 1994). Similarly, the United Villages of the Corner cooperative, which by 1990 represented 343 Zapotec coffee growers from the Sierra Juárez, had originally formed as part of a local

---

[16] On Oaxaca's ethnic diversity, see Barabás and Bartolomé 1986. The state's linguistic diversity is so broad that members of the same ethnic groups often speak mutually unintelligible dialects.

[17] The four regions were the Isthmus, the Mazateca, the Coast, and the Sierra Juárez. Among the ethnic groups were Chinanteco, Mazateco, Mixe, Mixteco, Triqui, Zapoteco, and Zoque (Aranda Bezaury 1992: 111).

[18] The Community Food Councils were part of the national Mexican Food System (SAM) initiative launched by President López Portillo in 1980. See Fox 1993.

struggle to secure rural roads and bus service for isolated, indigenous communities (author interview, June 1995).

By contrast, the 1,200–member Union of Indigenous Communities of the Isthmus (UCIRI), which was founded in the early 1980s by Jesuit priests, had focused on organic coffee production since its inception. UCIRI's clerical leadership instilled its Zapotec and Mixe rank and file with what might be called a "Jesuit work ethic," emphasizing producers' moral obligations to grow high-quality, organic coffee. From the start, UCIRI successfully tapped into European organic coffee markets with the help of Church-affiliated, agroecological organizations. The Isthmus region was also home to another major independent organization, the Union of Indigenous Communities of the Northern Isthmus. UCIZONI, which represented more than six hundred coffee producers, did not share UCIRI's religious focus; and despite their geographical proximity, the two organizations had little formal contact.

In sum, by 1988 several independent, yet isolated, producer organizations had emerged across Oaxaca. Indeed, these organizations might very well have remained dispersed had not Cantú's exclusionary project provided a common point of reference that led them to discover shared interests in gaining inclusion in the emerging post–INMECAFÉ policy regime.

Scaling Up: Birth of a Statewide Coordinating Network

In February 1989, Governor Ramírez organized a forum to unveil legislation that Cantú had drafted proposing a Law for the Promotion and Integral Development of Coffee Production in the State of Oaxaca (see Cantú Peña 1989). The forum, which was held in the town of Santiago Astata, proved to be a pivotal event in both the emergence of statewide opposition to Ramírez's neocorporatist project and the subsequent formation of a participatory policy regime.

Although the meeting was officially called the "First Statewide Forum for Study, Analysis, and Training about Coffee Production," its purpose was less to stimulate analysis and study than to demonstrate the coffee sector's support for the governor's project. According to several participants, the forum was intended as a "political show" staged mainly for invited representatives of various federal government agencies. One participant described the forum as "pre-cooked," pointing out that the official book, which supposedly summarized the conference's conclusions, had been prepared beforehand! (author interviews, December 1994). Not surprisingly, the forty-three organizations listed in the forum's program as representing small producers included only official organizations affiliated with the CNC. Independent organizations such as UCIZONI, UCI "Cien Años," and United Villages of the Corner were not invited (Moguel and Aranda 1992: 179; Ramírez Aguilar 1989a, 1989b).

The forum at Astata did not turn out as Ramírez and Cantú had expected. Although they had not been invited, leaders of independent organizations showed up anyway. Many had been tipped off about the event by a high-ranking official of a federal government social development agency, who believed that the post–INMECAFÉ policy arena should include independent organizations and urged them to attend the forum. Several of these uninvited leaders took the floor and expressed their opposition to the new legislation. Their criticisms focused especially on the composition of the proposed State Coffee Council, which, in their view, "implied the exclusion of broad sectors of producers from the council's management and decision-making processes" (quoted in Moguel and Aranda 1992: 180). They also criticized the legislation's proposal that the Coffee Council control export quotas and financing, which they saw as a threat to their organizations' primary economic objective: marketing their members' coffee.[19]

In addition to the immediate effect of fracturing the illusion of consensus that the state government had sought to create, the independent organizations' presence at Astata would soon have more profound consequences for Ramírez's neocorporatist program. At the forum, many of these independent organizations met for the first time, discovering their shared opposition to the governor's project. Their common status as illegitimate organizations in the eyes of the government helped foster a sense of collective identity. These initial contacts soon served as the basis for launching a statewide campaign against the governor's project.

The Astata conference also resulted in new linkages between the independent producer organizations and other actors who would become important allies in the subsequent struggle against the governor's neocorporatist initiative. INMECAFÉ field staff from across Oaxaca attended the conference as invited representatives of UEPCs. Some INMECAFÉ workers sought to end the traditional practice through which communities were compelled to accept leaders imposed by outside CNC officials insensitive to local needs. At Astata, many of these democratically inclined INMECAFÉ workers, who sought to ensure that producers could choose their own leaders, first learned about the independent organizations. They immediately recognized these organizations as attractive alternatives to the authori-

---

[19] The Astata forum was held six months prior to the rupture of the International Coffee Organization's (ICO) international quota system, after which control of export quotas became a moot issue.

tarian, usually corrupt CNC unions (author interviews, December 1994, May 1995).

These field workers would help integrate producers affiliated with INMECAFÉ's UEPCs into the process of constructing a new statewide organization, and their links to and legitimacy with UEPC communities contributed significantly to the rapid expansion of CEPCO's ranks. When their jobs with INMECAFÉ disappeared as its dismantling proceeded, many of these field workers became technical advisers to CEPCO or one of its affiliated regional organizations.

Thus, at the Astata forum the seeds were planted for the birth of a statewide producer organization opposed to the governor's neocorporatist project. Ironically, rather than demonstrating producer unity behind their project, as Ramírez and Cantú had planned, the forum served as the catalyst and point of departure for an opposition movement that would force its modification.

AFTER ASTATA

In the weeks following the Astata forum, the independent producer organizations embarked on an intense campaign of grassroots mobilization. They organized "alternative forums" in coffee-producing communities to discuss the state government's proposed legislation. Many producers not affiliated with an independent organization (such as members of INMECAFÉ's UEPCs) attended these forums; hence the meetings served to recruit new members. Modifying the governor's proposed legislation soon became the rallying point for thousands of small producers. Ramírez's neocorporatist project had thus inadvertently given the independent organizations both a stimulus to join forces and a useful tool with which to expand their bases of support.

The independent organizations also began to draft an alternative to Cantú's legislation. Their alternative rejected Cantú's proposal to grant the State Coffee Council control of export quotas and financing, a move that the independent organizations saw as an effort to roll back their hard-earned advances appropriating the coffee production process.[20] State control of export quotas had long been a source of rents and corruption for INMECAFÉ's employees as well as an important instrument for sustaining the CNC's monopoly in the coffee sector. State-controlled financing, in addition to providing further

---

[20] State control of export quotas and financing was part of the proposed "Fund to Guaranty and Defend Coffee Production." According to Cantú's proposal, the Fund, which would serve as the Coffee Council's "marketing and financing arm," would "administer the quotas corresponding to the production of coffee in Oaxaca" and would "manage and secure financial credits" for the sector. See Cantú Peña 1989.

opportunities for corruption, had forced producers to sell to IN-MECAFÉ, which offered advance credits in exchange for producers' commitments to repay the credit "in kind" with their harvests. As a document justifying the organizations' opposition to State Coffee Council control of financing bluntly put it, "[Cantú's proposal] would create a financial instrument—to control the money—that would be directed by a single individual who would not be chosen by the producers" (CEPCO 1989).

The independent organizations also proposed modifications to shift control of the State Coffee Council's Executive Committee from government agencies to the producers. As envisioned by Cantú, the nine-member Executive Committee would have included just two representatives of producers—the secretary general of the CNC's Agrarian Leagues and the president of the Oaxaca branch of the PRI's National Confederation of Smallholders (CNPP)—both members of the state-controlled corporatist framework. The rest of the committee would consist of state and federal government officials, with the governor serving as the committee's president (Cantú Peña 1989: 13).

The independent organizations proposed that the council's Executive Committee be expanded to include four representatives of small producer organizations, ten "at-large" representatives of producers drawn from each of Oaxaca's coffee regions, and two seats for private-sector industrialists and exporters. This change would have given a majority of votes to the producers' representatives.

Finally, the independent organizations sought to reduce the control of the Executive Committee's director—a post certain to be filled by Cantú. They proposed instead an Executive Council consisting of a general director, INMECAFÉ's delegate to Oaxaca, the state government's secretary of rural development, and the four representatives of small producer organizations to be incorporated into the expanded Executive Committee (CEPCO 1989; Moguel and Aranda 1992: 181).

After several months of grassroots consultation and mobilization, the independent organizations decided that the issues raised in their alternative forums should be discussed at a general meeting in the city of Oaxaca. This meeting, the First Forum of Consultation,[21] was held on June 2, 1989, in the auditorium of the National Education Workers Union (SNTE).

The meeting's location is significant because it reveals the close ties and mutual support between independent coffee organizations and Oaxaca's teachers' movement, which had been struggling for a decade to win internal union democratization.[22] The teachers' move-

---

[21] The full name was "The First Forum of Consultation Regarding the Problematic of Coffee in Oaxaca."

[22] On the teachers' movement, see Cook 1996.

ment had been a powerful political force in Oaxaca since the late 1970s, and Ramírez had spent much energy trying to subdue it. His efforts to co-opt some of the movement's leaders had indeed weakened the movement (Sorroza Polo 1994: 300). However, the prospects of a new coalition uniting teachers with coffee producers alarmed Ramírez.[23] Hence the threat of allying with the teachers greatly bolstered the producer organizations' bargaining strength, because it raised the costs to Ramírez of ignoring their demands and excluding them from the coffee-sector policy arena.

A large contingent of representatives of UEPCs attended the independent organizations' forum, reflecting the success of their recruitment efforts during the five months since the government's forum at Astata. The independent forum concluded with a strong condemnation of the governor's project, which was criticized as a scheme designed by bureaucrats and middlemen against the interests of "authentic small producers" (Castellanos 1989).

This productivist discourse, which framed the independent organizations as defenders of all small producers, facilitated the construction of a broad coalition. Indeed, the goal of modifying the governor's project partially transcended the official-independent divide. Productivist factions of the CNC (especially the State Union of Coffee Producers) opposed elements of Cantú's project, such as his plan for a quasi-public company—Oaxaca Pro-Export—that would monopolize coffee exports.[24] These CNC factions rejected this scheme because they viewed it as benefiting a small group of bureaucrats and private-sector elites at the expense of CNC rank and file. On several occasions, leaders of these CNC factions participated in the independent organizations' meetings, and the two groups joined forces in a tacit alliance against Cantú's proposed legislation (author interviews, April and May 1995).

Two weeks after the First Forum of Consultation, on June 15, the independent organizations held a larger meeting in Oaxaca City that included 335 delegates representing 105 UEPCs (CEPCO 1989). At this Second Forum, the independent organizations formalized their relationships by founding the Statewide Coordinating Network of Coffee Producers of Oaxaca.

Leaders of the recently created National Coordinating Network of Coffee Producers' Organizations (CNOC) attended the Second Forum and offered solidarity and key advice. The two organizing processes—CEPCO's at the state level and CNOC's at the national level—reinforced one another through valuable exchanges of information,

---

[23] This point was made by a former leader of the CNC's State Union of Coffee Producers (author interview, April 1995).

[24] On Oaxaca Pro-Export, see Gobierno 1989b.

experiences, and enthusiasm between the two newly formed organizations. In an effort to strengthen this mutual support dynamic, CNOC chose Oaxaca as the site for its first national meeting. The meeting, which was held in early July in the town of Lachiviza, brought together representatives of twenty-five independent coffee producer organizations from six states.

For CEPCO's members, CNOC's national meeting was an energizing experience that linked their local struggle to a larger, national movement. In the years to come, CNOC would provide much more to CEPCO than just inspiration and a sense of larger purpose. The national organization gave CEPCO—and other regional organizations like it—crucial leverage within the policy process by pressuring the central offices of federal government agencies in Mexico City. CNOC's direct access to central staff of federal agencies opened important new bargaining channels for subnational producer organizations like CEPCO.[25]

CEPCO CONSOLIDATES

During the rest of 1989, while continuing to oppose the governor's neocorporatist project, CEPCO expanded its focus to include economic development activities. The new organization began to articulate rank-and-file demands for government assistance to improve production infrastructure, obtaining a 500–million–peso grant from PRONASOL to finance the purchase of two thousand manual depulping machines.[26]

CEPCO also began to operate as a marketing cooperative through which producers could sell coffee at a higher price than that offered by either INMECAFÉ or private buyers. This new marketing role was partially thrust upon CEPCO by INMECAFÉ's drastic reduction of coffee purchases. For the 1989–1990 harvest, INMECAFÉ declared it would purchase a maximum of just 25 percent of Oaxaca's production and would only buy coffee that was almost fully processed (*pergamino seco*). The reduction of INMECAFÉ's purchasing quotas left thousands of small producers few options but to sell their harvests at exploitatively low prices to local middlemen. The crash of global coffee prices after the rupture of the International Coffee Organization's quota system in July 1989 exacerbated this difficult situation facing small producers.

This crisis situation proved an important resource for CEPCO. The intense uncertainty that Oaxaca's small producers faced created new

---

[25] On this aspect of CNOC, see Hernández 1992: 90–92.
[26] These machines separate the coffee cherry pulp from the bean inside.

opportunities for independent organizations to expand their ranks by incorporating producers who had previously depended on INMECAFÉ. CEPCO soon began to substitute for INMECAFÉ in various ways, undertaking core activities such as credit management, harvesting, processing, and national and international marketing.[27]

These efforts to take control of the production process were supported by middle- and high-level federal government officials, who channeled resources to CEPCO via PRONASOL. In late 1989, the organization received a loan of two million pesos through the newly formed INI–PRONASOL Program for Coffee Harvesting and Marketing (Gracida, Guzmán, and Moreno 1990). This loan enabled CEPCO to purchase coffee at competitive prices. The same federal official who had previously informed the independent organizations about the Astata forum also played a pivotal role in securing this loan (author interviews, December 1994 and June 1995). Prior to the presidential election of 1988, this official had participated in a successful campaign to garner tacit endorsements for the PRI's candidate, Carlos Salinas de Gortari, from Oaxaca's independent producer organizations by securing their signatures on neutral-sounding newspaper advertisements.[28] Hence CEPCO was reaping the rewards of the decision not to oppose Salinas's candidacy made by some of its major constituent organizations during the previous year's elections.

In less than a year, CEPCO had evolved from a loose social movement into a full-blown campesino enterprise uniting 20,000 small producers. This transformation, which was supported in crucial ways by reformist federal government officials, ensured that CEPCO would not fade away after it had won the struggle to modify Ramírez's neocorporatist project. On the contrary, CEPCO would endure as a pivotal player in the post–INMECAFÉ policy arena.

---

[27] In 1990, CEPCO's organizations were able to offer a price of 3,200 pesos per kilo, 450 pesos above INMECAFÉ's price of 2,764 pesos (Moguel and Aranda 1992: 184).

[28] See, for example, *La Jornada* 1988. Independent coffee producer organizations from Oaxaca that signed the document included the UCI "Cien Años" and the United Villages of the Corner of the Sierra Juárez. See also the open letter to Salinas de Gortari from "autonomous, self-managed peasant organizations from the state of Oaxaca," which affirmed support for Salinas's emphasis on respecting these organizations' autonomy from corporatist ruling-party confederations and on transferring productive functions from the public sector to the producers. In addition to the two organizations mentioned above, this second advertisement was also signed by the UCI-ZONI, which, together with UCI "Cien Años" and United Villages, would play a central role in CEPCO's formation in 1989 (*La Jornada*, June 30, 1988).

Designing the State Coffee Council

In October 1989 the state legislature of Oaxaca finally sent the governor's proposed coffee-sector legislation for review by its Agriculture, Forest, and Mines Committee. This action shifted the attention of independent producer organizations to the legislative review process. CEPCO soon launched a campaign to gather petitions expressing opposition to the legislation. The campaign yielded more than 20,000 signed petitions, which were soon delivered to the legislature. Influencing the legislature, however, was not the main objective, because it was little more than the governor's rubber stamp. As one of CEPCO's leaders explained, "the point [of the petition campaign] was not to impress the legislators. It was to make the governor take note of our strength" (author interview, March 1995).

CEPCO's leaders also attended the meetings of the Agriculture, Forest, and Mines Committee and participated actively in its analysis of the legislation. In early December, CEPCO finally secured formal recognition by the state government, when its leaders were officially invited to participate in a legislative forum to analyze and modify the governor's proposal. The modified legislation was finally approved on February 6, 1990, fourteen months after Ramírez had first sent it to the legislature.

A comparison of the final legislation (Gobierno 1990) with Cantú's (1989) original proposal reveals the significant achievements of the producer movement. First, Cantú's proposal that the State Coffee Council control marketing and financing through a Fund for the Defense and Guaranty of Coffee Production was watered down considerably.[29] Although the final legislation did stipulate the fund's creation, it was designed as a voluntary scheme. Few producers chose to participate, and the fund was never established.

Regarding the structure of representation within the Coffee Council, the final legislation expanded the Executive Committee to include four additional seats for nongovernmental organizations, one of which was specifically designated for CEPCO's president. Cantú's original proposal had granted just two Executive Committee seats to producer organizations (the CNC and CNPP), compared with six seats for government officials. The modification to the structure of the Executive Committee, which established an even distribution of seats between governmental and nongovernmental actors, reflected CEPCO's demand that the Coffee Council include greater representation of producers. Although CEPCO's proposal that the council include ten at-large representatives from Oaxaca's coffee regions was rejected, the legislation did leave the door open for producers to in-

---

[29] The issue of who would control export quotas was now moot; see note 20.

crease their weight within the council through a provision that any legally constituted producer organization could be incorporated with the council's approval.[30] Furthermore, the important power to convoke extraordinary council meetings, which in the original proposal had been restricted to the council's president (that is, to the governor), was expanded to include the "coffee producers represented in the council" (Gobierno 1990).

The final legislation did not include CEPCO's proposal to limit the power of the Executive Committee's director by establishing an Executive Council of four representatives from producer organizations. However, fears that the director would monopolize power and block producer participation were assuaged by the governor's decision to dismiss Cantú. The new director, a local coffee producer, soon demonstrated a firm commitment to include all producer organizations in the Coffee Council. His frank, consensus-seeking style and honest reputation would prove critical in the council's subsequent successes and consolidation.

In sum, CEPCO had accomplished a remarkable goal. In little over a year, the producer organization had transformed itself from an officially unrecognized, excluded actor into a legitimate, autonomous force in a new State Coffee Council it had helped design.

The Participatory Policy Regime: Government-Producer Collaboration in the State Coffee Council

The thousands of small producers who struggled for inclusion in Oaxaca's new institutions for coffee-sector governance obviously valued the ability to participate in policy decisions that affected their lives. However, Oaxaca's participatory policy regime gave them much more than just a voice in the policy process—the new State Coffee Council played an important developmental role, promoting the competitiveness of Oaxaca's coffee and the economic welfare of its small producers.

Participation by producer organizations enabled the council to play this positive role by helping it secure crucial collective goods, such as a large share of the government's budget as well as development projects that responded to the producers' needs and yielded significant advances in productivity and quality. The organizations' ongoing involvement in the council also served as the basis for a new, promotional strategy of development that targeted public resources

---

[30] Several new organizations would soon gain seats within the council, including two former CEPCO affiliates that withdrew from the organization.

to support and augment the organizations' existing capacities. Rather than competing with grassroots organizations and duplicating the important activities they performed (such as marketing), as had INMECAFÉ, the Coffee Council sought instead to complement the producer organizations, mixing their social capital with its state capital through collaborative developmental joint ventures.[31]

These partnerships between producer organizations and government combined the formers' local knowledge, hands-on experience, and infrastructure with the latter's financial resources and technical expertise. Given the requirement of fiscal constraint imposed by national neoliberal policies, these government-producer partnerships proved to be effective, low-cost tools for promoting economic development.

Provision of Collective Goods

Oaxaca's State Coffee Council achieved a high degree of centrality in the interactions between producer organizations and both federal and state government agencies. The council functioned as an almost exclusive window through which producer organizations channeled demands and negotiated policies and projects.

The council also served as a forum where the diverse interest groups in Oaxaca's coffee sector mobilized consensus on public policy issues. This consensus, combined with the council's centrality, increased the coffee sector's weight within the larger public policy arena: by channeling demands collectively through the council, Oaxaca's producer organizations presented a united front to the multiple state and federal agencies in charge of rural policy and programs. The ability to present a unified front yielded especially large returns during the annual fiscal appropriations process.

Furthermore, the Coffee Council operated as a kind of policy antechamber, where the coffee sector put its own house in order by deciding its needs and how public resources for the sector should be spent. Once consensus and clarity were reached on these issues, the council's technical staff worked together with the technical advisers of producer organizations to draft proposals for programs and projects chosen by the organizations. Consequently, the council's director could lobby government officials in charge of planning and budgeting equipped not only with the unified support of the producer organizations but also with solid, crisp policy proposals in hand. The

---

[31] On social capital, see Putnam 1993; Evans 1996a, 1996b.

steady annual growth of the council's budget illustrates the success of these lobbying efforts.[32]

After the State Planning Commission of Oaxaca (COPLADE) had established the coffee sector's annual budget, the Coffee Council would meet to decide how programmed funds should be distributed across the menu of projects previously chosen by producer organizations. At this stage, leaders of the producer organizations also decided how projects would be distributed among organizations.

This latter phase of the planning process was always quite contentious because the collective objective of securing as much money as possible for the sector as a whole, which had previously united the organizations, was now supplanted by each organization's individual goal of guaranteeing the largest possible share of the overall project pie for its constituents. In addition to the obvious barriers to consensus created by this situation, strong pressures also emerged for an economically inefficient, pork-barrel pattern of project distribution characterized by unnecessary duplication and redundancy, especially in regions and communities cohabited by rival organizations.

At this stage, the Coffee Council's staff and director supplied an important collective good by performing a disciplinary role that defused the potential for pork-barrel project distribution. The council's *micro-bodega* program of very small storehouses exemplifies how this disciplinary role helped prevent inefficient, wasteful use of scarce public resources. The council's staff prepared a list of all localities where competing organizations (typically a CEPCO affiliate and a CNC affiliate) had made overlapping requests for micro-bodegas. The council's director contacted the leaders of the rival organizations, informing them that it was not possible to construct more than one *bodega* (storehouse) per community and that they would either have to agree to share a single expanded bodega or receive none. The council would fund construction of a partition to divide the expanded bodega into separate compartments. Faced with these options, most disputing organizations soon agreed that part of a big bodega was better than none. Hence the council's director prevented unnecessary project duplication and, displaying his talent for inducing consensus, devised a solution that compelled rival organizations to learn to live together.[33]

The council also delivered an important collective good by helping insulate the planning and resource allocation processes from the effects of conjunctural political pressures, which often strongly influenced public planning in Oaxaca. When asked to compare the coffee

---

[32] For example, between 1993 and 1994, the council's total budget increased sixfold, from 22.4 million pesos to 120.6 million pesos. See Consejo 1994a.

[33] Based on author observations, December 1994; and Consejo 1994b.

sector with other sectors, one top state-government planning official candidly responded that public resources were typically allocated in a haphazard, case-by-case fashion and that the organizations that "shouted the loudest" usually benefited most. In the coffee sector, by contrast, he noted that the coordination and consensus achieved by producer organizations through the Coffee Council helped insulate government planners from the volatility of short-run political pressures, yielding long-term, integrated programs that addressed real developmental needs rather than conjunctural political issues (author interview, June 1995).

The Coffee Council's program for controlling pests and parasites exemplifies both provision of collective goods and the strategy of establishing developmental partnerships with producer organizations. In 1993 the council founded a Regional Plant Sanitation Committee. The principal challenge confronting this committee's staff of agronomists was a growing infestation of Oaxaca's coffee fields by the broca beetle.[34] By 1994 the broca plague had affected an estimated 45,000 of Oaxaca's 174,000 hectares of coffee, jeopardizing the livelihoods of roughly 10,000 producers across the state.[35] If unchecked, the plague threatened to damage the state's entire production.

Because of the broca plague's magnitude and the Plant Sanitation Committee's modest resources, the committee alone could not have begun to control the infestation. In the context of these resource constraints, a top-down, INMECAFÉ–style solution that relied on standardized, mass-produced technical packages distributed directly to producers was not possible. Fortunately, the committee had other options. In the wake of INMECAFÉ's withdrawal and the elimination of most state-provided technical assistance, many of the producer organizations had, by necessity, hired their own technical advisers.[36] Hence, by 1993, the most important producer organizations had acquired formidable in-house technical expertise which, as the committee's staff recognized, could be deployed to combat the broca plague.

In the design and implementation of the anti-broca campaign, the Plant Sanitation Committee focused its energies where it could achieve the most value added: training the organizations' technical staff in the best techniques for combating the plague, as well as coordinating and disseminating results of academic research to monitor

---

[34] The broca beetle bores into the coffee cherry, destroying the bean. Coffee rust was also a problem in Oaxaca.

[35] Escalante Durán, Ruiz Vega, and Rojo Soberanes 1994. The broca was first detected in Oaxaca in 1989, when it was estimated to have affected 28,000 hectares.

[36] Indeed, many of these advisers were prior INMECAFÉ employees who had lost their jobs due to its dismantling.

and improve plague control.[37] Furthermore, the committee drew the organizations' technical advisers as well as their rank and file into the research process, promoting their participation in data collection. Eliciting producer organizations' involvement in the anti-broca campaign made sense because of the important local knowledge their members could provide regarding climatic and biological conditions.

Local variations in factors such as altitude and humidity have important impacts on the severity of broca infestation. Such variations also influence the effectiveness of different strategies for combating broca. For example, university researchers discovered that the *Beauveria bassiana* mushroom, which poisons broca beetles when distributed in soil under coffee plants, worked most effectively in areas of high humidity.[38] The detailed knowledge producers could provide about local production conditions helped ensure adoption of the most appropriate strategy for fighting the broca plague.

The public sector thus fashioned a new role for itself in Oaxaca. In contrast to the old INMECAFÉ model of massive, top-down intervention, the Coffee Council's Plant Sanitation Committee functioned like a public-service consulting firm, training the organizations' own technicians in the best methods for managing the broca problem. Furthermore, the committee promoted development of better technologies for plague control by linking academic researchers with producer organizations. And by drawing producers into the process of fighting the broca, the Coffee Council's plant sanitation program helped transform them from passive recipients of mass-produced technical packages into active agents with important roles to play in protecting their own livelihoods.

Government-Producer Joint Ventures

The Coffee Council developed an innovative strategy to promote the welfare and market competitiveness of Oaxaca's small coffee producers by complementing their organizations' existing capabilities and incorporating them into planning and implementation of development projects. This government-producer collaboration yielded tar-

---

[37] For example, the Plant Sanitation Committee disseminated the findings of a team of university researchers from the Autonomous Technological Institute of Oaxaca (ITAO), which identified an important local source of the *Beauveria bassiana* mushroom, an especially effective agent for fighting broca. The Committee also published a bimonthly newsletter; one issue was devoted almost entirely to results of government-supported research on strategies for controlling the broca.

[38] In conditions of high humidity, the mushroom spores, when ingested by a broca beetle, reproduce on the cadaver of the poisoned beetle and infect other beetles (Córdoba Gamez 1994).

geted, low-cost programs that responded to producers' needs and promised significant advances in productivity and quality.

The micro-bodega project exemplifies this strategy of forming government-producer joint ventures. The project's goal was to construct bodegas in seventy-three communities in order to benefit more than ten thousand small coffee producers.[39] Each bodega was designed to hold up to four hundred bags of semi-processed, "pergamino" coffee and would improve quality by providing regulated humidity and protecting recently harvested beans from natural adversities.

The official project planning document emphasized how lack of adequate short-term storage facilities seriously limited the ability of Oaxaca's small producers to compete in export markets. This document further justified the micro-bodega project as an effective way for the public sector to complement and strengthen the marketing and processing infrastructure owned by producer organizations. According to the document, "The organizations will have considerable savings with regard to transport costs because they will no longer have to purchase coffee directly in each community, but rather at the [micro-bodega] collection centers. These will be strategically located in each coffee-producing zone so that collection will occur in large quantities rather than with small jeeps traveling community by community" (Consejo 1995a). The document also explains how the micro-bodegas would benefit the organizations by helping guarantee a reliable supply of primary materials for their agro-industrial infrastructure. Indeed, the document explicitly acknowledges the producer organizations as the source of the initial project proposal.

The implementation of the micro-bodega project further illustrates government-producer collaboration. In the spirit of "co-responsibility" between the public sector and beneficiaries of government programs, the Coffee Council's staff restricted its role to designing the bodegas, administering project funds, and providing technical supervision.[40] The rank and file of producer organizations supplied the construction materials and labor.

The micro-bodega project was a collaborative, low-cost program designed to help plug an important leak in the coffee production process identified by Oaxaca's small producer organizations: inadequate short-term storage facilities. The project promised to boost their abilities to compete in global markets by reducing transportation and processing costs and improving quality.

---

[39] Each bodega would measure 5 by 8 meters.

[40] The idea of co-responsibility was a central component of the national PRONASOL program.

Another important collaborative project was the construction of nearly three thousand small-scale, wet-processing plants across 165 communities. These processing plants, each of which consisted of a small tank for washing and fermenting depulped coffee beans as well as concrete patios for drying them, were simple and inexpensive to build. In contrast to a micro-bodega, which benefited approximately 135 producers, the wet-processing plants were "family-sized" agro-industry, designed for just one or two producers and their families. Like the micro-bodegas, however, the wet-processing facilities were cheap and highly effective solutions to problems of productivity and quality.

The council's justification for the processing plant project resembled that for the micro-bodega project: promoting the ability of small producer organizations to compete in export markets by improving coffee quality and reducing production costs. The official document summarizing the project articulated the council's goal of buttressing and augmenting the producer organizations' existing capacities: "Given the organizations' experience in harvesting, processing, and marketing, this project seeks to expand their ability to operate in the external market because good processing guarantees good quality, which, in turn, boosts market competitiveness" (Consejo 1995b). The project's ultimate goal was to increase Oaxaca's overall production of export-quality coffee by 15 percent (from 75 to 90 percent of total production).

The small-scale processing plants appealed to producers because the new infrastructure would enable them to increase the value of their product. This family-sized agro-industry promised significant gains in the price small producers could command for their crops, since the wet-processing stage critically affects coffee quality. Unprocessed coffee cherries start to decompose within twenty-four hours of picking; because of Oaxaca's rugged, mountainous terrain, small farmers often had difficulty getting freshly picked cherries to a wet-processing plant within this time limit. In many cases, producers owned small, hand-cranked depulpers, but they lacked tanks to ferment and wash the depulped beans, washing them instead in crude, unsanitary plastic basins. Another important source of quality losses was the lack of concrete patios for drying washed beans, a situation frequently resolved by drying coffee in the dirt. The official project document bluntly summarized the end result of these various deficiencies in wet-processing infrastructure: "bad taste in the cup."[41]

---

[41] Consejo 1995b. According to the document, approximately 50,000 of Oaxaca's small and midsize producers lacked sufficient infrastructure to guarantee the quality of their product.

In addition to improving quality, the wet-processing plants promised large efficiency gains for producer organizations because their truck fleets would no longer have to transport unprocessed coffee, with its dead weight of pulp, mucilage, and honey, from the communities to centralized processing factories. Because on-site wet processing reduced total weight by a factor of approximately four, these efficiency gains were considerable.[42] Furthermore, producers could use the coffee pulp as compost and organic fertilizer. Hence it made little sense to transport pulp out of their communities. Finally, the family-sized processing plants avoided the massive environmental contamination caused by runoff from centralized, large-scale facilities.

The wet-processing plant and micro-bodega projects exemplify how Oaxaca's participatory policy regime supported demand-based projects solicited by grassroots organizations and implemented through government-producer partnerships. In these partnerships, the public sector made strategic contributions of technical expertise and money to help fill gaps in the production process through which quality and competitiveness were lost. The producer organizations identified these gaps, providing the crucial information base for the public sector's targeted interventions, and they played the central roles in project implementation.

Conclusion: Institutional Innovation along Corporatist Lines

The case of Oaxaca illustrates how powerful grassroots organizations can transform exclusionary corporatist institutions into participatory policy regimes. In Oaxaca, a neocorporatist project intended to strengthen authoritarian modes of policy making supplied institutional raw materials that a grassroots movement reworked into a participatory framework that benefited small coffee producers. The State Coffee Council, which formed the heart of Oaxaca's participatory policy regime, served as an arena for mobilizing consensus among competing interests in the coffee sector and for forging government-producer collaborations. These collaborative projects creatively combined producer organizations' social capital with govern-

---

[42] It takes 245 kilograms of coffee cherry to produce 57.5 kilograms of dry pergamino (the product of wet processing). The pergamino must then be dry-processed to produce green coffee (*café oro*).

ment's state capital in ways that improved the ability of small coffee farmers to compete in the global marketplace.[43]

Politicians with state-building proclivities seem to be a necessary ingredient for participatory policy regimes. Such politicians try to win support and manage imperatives of incumbency by constructing new public institutions and expanding the role of government. These new institutions, in turn, may provide incentives and focal points that trigger and help sustain mobilization by societal groups. As exemplified by the case of Oaxaca, the combination of institution building from above and organized pressure from below can result in participatory policy regimes.

The populist government of Oaxaca supplied the institutional raw materials that grassroots producer organizations made into a participatory policy regime. Oaxaca's governor at the time INMECAFÉ withdrew was a relic from a bygone era of statist policies, and he surrounded himself with advisers who shared his political and ideological formation. In terms of their policy preferences and perceptions of the public sector's appropriate economic role, the officials who launched the neocorporatist project in Oaxaca were a far cry from the neoliberals in Mexico City who championed market-oriented reform. Nor were these officials insulated technocrats motivated by technical policy goals and ideological blueprints. The neocorporatist initiative in Oaxaca was driven instead by the overtly political objective of strengthening the government's support base.

However, state-building politicians who launch neocorporatist projects should not be considered sufficient conditions for participatory policy regimes. In the absence of coordinated pressure from below, such projects will likely result in old-style, state-controlled corporatist arrangements that serve more to generate political support than to promote economic performance. Mobilized societal groups with the incentives and capacity to rework neocorporatist institutions and hold government officials accountable are also necessary conditions for participatory policy regimes.

Furthermore, in order for participatory policy regimes to foster the kinds of government-producer partnerships seen in Oaxaca, producer organizations should be capable of more than just lodging demands, pressuring for inclusion, and monitoring government performance; they should also be committed to shouldering new economic responsibilities. The State Coffee Council of Oaxaca succeeded in curtailing costly externalities because producer organizations participated vigorously in its programs to recycle environmen-

---

[43] On the strikingly different performance of the coffee councils in the states of Guerrero, Puebla, and Chiapas, which for the most part failed to deliver the benefits enjoyed by Oaxaca's small producers, see Snyder 1999a, n.d.

tally hazardous production by-products (such as the pulp of coffee cherries). By helping control free-rider problems in the management of parasites and pests, producer organizations played a crucial auxiliary role that buttressed the Coffee Council's efforts to "police the commons." Finally, by assuming primary responsibility for marketing crops, the organizations freed government agencies to focus on the area where they could contribute the most value added: targeted interventions to plug leaks in the production process through which quality and productivity were lost.

Oaxaca's producer organizations thus did much more than just pressure and shout. They also embraced new economic roles (like self-management of production and marketing) that formed the basis for novel divisions of labor between producers and government that harnessed the comparative strengths of each. Together with state-building politicians, engaged productivist organizations able to defend their interests by challenging government policy, yet committed to self-management of core economic activities, seem basic components of participatory policy regimes.

References

Aranda Bezaury, Josefina. 1992. "Camino andado, retos y propuestas: la Coordinadora Estatal de Productores de Café de Oaxaca," *Cuadernos del Sur* 1 (2): 89–112.

Barabás, Alicia, and Miguel Bartolomé, eds. 1986. *Etnicidad y pluralismo cultural: la dinámica étnica en Oaxaca*. Mexico City: Instituto Nacional de Antropología e Historia.

Cantú Peña, Fausto. 1989. "Proyecto de ley para el fomento y desarrollo integral de la caficultura en el estado de Oaxaca." In *Primer encuentro estatal de estudio, análisis y capacitación sobre caficultura*. Oaxaca: Secretaría de Desarrollo Rural, Gobierno del Estado de Oaxaca.

Castellanos, Luis. 1989. "Caficultores condenan la iniciativa de ley de caficultura," *Extra de Oaxaca*, June 2.

CEPCO (Coordinadora Estatal de Productores de Café de Oaxaca). 1989. *El Cosechero* 1 (1).

Consejo Estatal del Café del Estado de Oaxaca. 1994a. "Resumen de inversión por proyectos."

———. 1994b. "Relación de obras agroindustriales duplicadas por diferente organización en una misma localidad."

———. 1995a. "Construcción de microbodegas rurales para acopio de café."

———. 1995b. "Construcción de microbeneficios húmedos, ciclo 1995."

Cook, Maria Lorena. 1996. *Organizing Dissent: Unions, the State, and the Democratic Teachers' Movement in Mexico*. University Park: Pennsylvania State University Press.

Córdoba Gamez, Gabriel. 1994. "Avances del control biológico contra la broca del fruto del cafeto a partir del hongo *Beauveria bassiana*," *Gaceta Fitosanitaria* 2: 4–7.

Cornelius, Wayne A., Ann L. Craig, and Jonathan Fox. 1994. "Mexico's National Solidarity Program: An Overview." In *Transforming State-Society Relations in Mexico: The National Solidarity Strategy*, edited by Wayne A. Cornelius, Ann L. Craig, and Jonathan Fox. La Jolla: Center for U.S.–Mexican Studies, University of California, San Diego.

Díaz Cárdenas, Salvador, Conrado Márquez Rosano, et al. 1991. "El sistema agroindustrial café y sus perspectivas." In *Memoria del II Seminario Nacional sobre la Agroindustria en México: Alternativa para el Desarrollo Agroindustrial*. Vol. 1. Chapingo: Universidad Autónoma Chapingo.

Escalante Durán, Carlos, Jaime Ruiz Vega, and Jorge Rojo Soberanes. 1994. "Pérdidas causadas por la broca del fruto del cafeto (*Hypothenemus hampei*) durante las etapas de producción y beneficiado del grano," *Gaceta Fitosanitaria* 2: 8–9.

Evans, Peter. 1996a. "Introduction: Development Strategies across the Public-Private Divide," *World Development* 24 (6): 1033–37.

————. 1996b. "Government Action, Social Capital and Development: Reviewing the Evidence on Synergy," *World Development* 24 (6): 1119–32.

Fox, Jonathan. 1993. *The Politics of Food in Mexico: State Power and Social Mobilization*. Ithaca, N.Y.: Cornell University Press.

————. 1996. "How Does Civil Society Thicken? The Political Construction of Social Capital in Rural Mexico," *World Development* 24 (6): 1089–1103.

Fox, Jonathan, and Gustavo Gordillo. 1989. "Between State and Market: The Campesinos' Quest for Autonomy." In *Mexico's Alternative Political Futures*, edited by Wayne A. Cornelius, Judith Gentleman, and Peter H. Smith. La Jolla: Center for U.S.–Mexican Studies, University of California, San Diego.

Gobierno del Estado de Oaxaca. 1989a. *Primer Encuentro Estatal de Estudio, Análisis y Capacitación sobre Cafeticultura*. Oaxaca: Secretaría de Desarrollo Rural.

————. 1989b. Decreto Num. 8. *Periódico Oficial* 71 (August 7).

————. 1990. Decreto Num. 27. *Periódico Oficial* 72 (April 4).

————. 1992a. *Del Oaxaca mágico al encuentro con la modernidad: seis años de transformación y desarrollo, 1986–1992, marco legislativo*.

————. 1992b. *Del Oaxaca mágico al encuentro con la modernidad: seis años de transformación y desarrollo, 1986–1992, resumen general*.

Gracida, Cecilia, Armando Guzmán, and Carlos Moreno. 1990. "Solidaridad en Oaxaca: una experiencia de concertación con los productores de café." Mimeo.

Hernández, Luis. 1992. "Cafetaleros: del adelgazamiento estatal a la guerra del mercado." In *Autonomía y nuevos sujetos sociales en el desarrollo rural*, edited by Julio Moguel, Carlota Botey, and Luis Hernández. Mexico City: Siglo Veintiuno.

La Jornada. 1988. "A la opinión pública," July 2.

Martínez Vásquez, Víctor Raúl. 1990. *Movimiento popular y política en Oaxaca: 1968–1986*. Mexico City: Consejo National para la Cultura y las Artes.

Moguel, Julio, and Josefina Aranda. 1992. "Los nuevos caminos en la construcción de la autonomía: la experiencia de la Coordinadora Estatal de Productores de Café de Oaxaca." In *Autonomía y nuevos sujetos sociales en el desarrollo rural,* edited by Julio Moguel, Carlota Botey, and Luis Hernández. Mexico City: Siglo Veintiuno.

Putnam, Robert. 1993. *Making Democracy Work: Civic Traditions in Modern Italy.* Princeton, N.J.: Princeton University Press.

Ramírez Aguilar, Fausto. 1989a. "Astata y la cafeticultura," *Extra de Oaxaca,* February 2.

———. 1989b. "Los subjetivos acuerdos de Astata," *Extra de Oaxaca,* February 4.

Rubin, Jeffrey W. 1996. "Decentering the Regime: Culture and Regional Politics in Mexico," *Latin American Research Review* 31 (3): 85–126.

Snyder, Richard. 1999a. "After Neoliberalism: The Politics of Reregulation in Mexico," *World Politics* 51 (2): 173–204.

———. 1999b. "After the State Withdraws: Neoliberalism and Subnational Authoritarian Regimes in Mexico." In *Subnational Politics and Democratization in Mexico,* edited by Wayne A. Cornelius, Todd A. Eisenstadt, and Jane Hindley. La Jolla: Center for U.S.–Mexican Studies, University of California, San Diego.

———. n.d. "Politics after Neoliberalism: Reregulation in Mexico, 1985–1995." Manuscript.

Sorroza Polo, Carlos J. 1994. "Oaxaca." In *La República Mexicana: modernización y democracia de Aguascalientes a Zacatecas,* edited by Pablo González Casanova and Jorge Cadena Roa. Vol. 2. Mexico City: Centro de Investigaciones Interdisciplinarias en Humanidades, Universidad Nacional Autónoma de México.

Villarreal, René. 1993. *Liberalismo social y reforma del estado: México en la era del capitalismo posmoderno.* Mexico City: Fondo de Cultura Económica.

Yescas Martínez, Isidoro. 1991. *Política y poder en Oaxaca: la sucesión gubernamental de 1986.* Oaxaca: Dirección de Comunicación Social del Gobierno del Estado de Oaxaca.

4

The New Top-Down Organizing: Campesino Coffee Growers in the Chatino Region of Oaxaca

Jorge Hernández Díaz

Coffee production plays an important role in the Mexican economy. In 1989, coffee exports were Mexico's third most important source of foreign exchange.[1] Between January and November 1996, coffee exports from Oaxaca earned U.S.$8,371,000 and accounted for 22 percent of that state's exports (SECOFI 1997: 8). Over 60,000 of Oaxaca's small farmers and their families work directly in coffee production, and recent changes in both domestic and international policy have affected them dramatically.

Faced with this new environment, Oaxaca's coffee growers have responded by organizing themselves in different ways to increase output, experiment with new production techniques, and diversify their markets in the hope of raising their incomes and improving their standard of living. These developments have been widely analyzed. Most studies have focused on the actions taken by independ-

This chapter is based largely on interviews with directors of coffee producer organizations and their rank and file, as well as with officials from government agencies in the region under study. Fieldwork was conducted by Mirna Cruz and the author between August 1996 and March 1997 in the Chatino region of Oaxaca State, supported in part by the Center for U.S.–Mexican Studies at the University of California, San Diego. The author thanks Richard Snyder, Horacio Mackinlay, and Josefina Aranda for their helpful comments. Translation by Patricia Rosas.

[1] Martínez Morales (1997) provides an exhaustive review of coffee production, marketing, and industrialization in Mexico.

ent organizations that have challenged the state's corporatist structure and experimented with novel production and marketing techniques. Such is the case with the Union of Indigenous Communities of the Isthmus (UCIRI), a regional organization promoted by members of the clergy sympathetic to liberation theology. In Oaxaca, members of UCIRI were pioneers in the production techniques for growing coffee organically, and they have been enormously successful because of contacts with European markets (Vazques and Villagómez 1993; Hernández Díaz 1995). Another example is the Statewide Coordinating Network of Coffee Producers of Oaxaca (CEPCO), an organization that comprises most of the local and regional coffee grower organizations in Oaxaca that are not affiliated with the government-controlled National Peasants' Confederation (CNC). In turn, CEPCO has joined the National Coordinating Network of Coffee Producers' Organizations (CNOC) (Moguel, Botey, and Hernández 1992; Hernández 1991; Aranda 1992).

According to a census taken by the government of Oaxaca's State Coffee Council (Consejo Estatal del Café), 49,800 small farmers belonged to growers' associations in 1994: 22,740 were affiliated with CEPCO and 18,842 with the National Peasants' Confederation. The remainder belonged to local-level organizations but were not affiliated with regional- or national-level associations. Recently, most of these farmers have joined a new government-sponsored organization, the Union of Indigenous Coffee Producers' Organizations (UOPICAFE).

This chapter attempts to document what has gone on among coffee growers who organized primarily at the urging of the government, a group that existing studies have largely ignored. The chapter focuses on the experiences of campesinos affiliated with three organizations—Kyat-ñuu, Chatinna, and Shalyuu-Kia—which, in turn, are members of the Chatinos Unidos Union, a regional organization that is part of UOPICAFE and comprises almost 3,000 small farmers.

Through their organizing efforts, members of the Chatinos Unidos Union and the UOPICAFE have to some degree managed to avoid middlemen, and that has made it possible for them to forge more direct links to the international market. Membership in these producer organizations has also given the small coffee farmers valuable experience in managing loans and in controlling resources needed to start collective production projects. The strategies that produced these accomplishments are similar to those followed by independent organizations. Like them, the government-sponsored organizations affiliated with UOPICAFE have launched programs for food distribution and credit, as well as for the reassertion of indigenous identity through a resuscitation of cultural traditions and a demand for respect for the region's culture.

Coffee and the Chatinos

Since its inception during the last third of the nineteenth century, coffee cultivation in Mexico has been closely tied to the international market (Rojas 1964; Romero 1886). Today Mexico exports between 80 and 90 percent of its coffee crop.[2] Coffee is grown in twelve states in central and southern Mexico, but four states—Chiapas, Veracruz, Oaxaca, and Puebla—together produce 80 percent or more of Mexico's total output (Nolasco 1985). Oaxaca ranks second in Mexico for the number of coffee growers and land area dedicated to coffee production. Calculated in terms of total production, the most important coffee-producing regions in Oaxaca are the Coast (Costa) and the Southern Highlands (Sierra Sur). The Coast comprises the districts of Jamiltepec, Pochutla, and Juquila.[3] This chapter focuses on the last of these districts, which includes most of the Chatino population.

The Chatino region in southeastern Oaxaca covers primarily eight of twelve municipalities in the district of Juquila and one (of fifteen) in the district of Sola de Vega. The Chatinos are one of sixteen indigenous groups in Oaxaca. They live in an area that covers approximately 2,000 square kilometers, and they share the mountains of the Pacific Coast of Oaxaca with people of mestizo blood who speak only Spanish. Currently, the Chatinos number about 38,000, most of whom reside in nine municipalities which are also home to about 5,000 mestizos.[4]

In the second half of the nineteenth century, during the period known in Mexican history as the Reform, domestic and foreign capitalists took over a large part of the Chatino lands, which until then had been communal property. The federal government, in its effort to consolidate Mexico's national economy, promoted both domestic and foreign capital investments in the "land in dead hands": the property

---

[2] Mexico became an important coffee exporter after 1950 and reached its peak productivity with the 1988–1989 harvest (Piñón Jiménez 1995). Since that time, production has dropped considerably. The most dramatic losses occurred with the 1993–1994 crop as a result of the drastic decline in global coffee prices.

[3] The state of Oaxaca comprises 570 municipalities, divided into 30 political-administrative districts, many of them matching the boundaries of the old political units recognized during the Porfiriato.

[4] The zone in which most of the Chatino-speaking people live covers the municipalities of San Miguel Panixtlahuaca, San Juan Lachao, Santos Reyes Nopala, Santa María Temaxcaltepec, Santa Catarina Juquila, San Juan Quiahije, Santiago Yaitepec, Tataltepec de Valdez, and Santa María Zenzontepec. Of its total area, about 65 percent is mountains ranging in altitude from 400 to 2,500 meters above sea level, 30 percent is small valleys and canyons (which is the best land for coffee cultivation), and the remaining 5 percent is low-land steppe.

of the Catholic Church and indigenous communities. In response,
Mexican businessmen and later foreign investors, primarily Germans,
took over some of the Chatino lands and began to plant coffee. This
new form of landholding was consolidated during the 1930s and
1940s. Thus a division was established, with the owners of the huge
coffee plantations on one side and the small farmers with communally held lands on the other. With the exception of the large coffee
plantations, or *fincas*, all land in the Chatino region today is held
communally.

Since the founding of the coffee plantations, the Chatinos have
participated in the economy as manual laborers. Much of the indigenous population works on the fincas seasonally, from October to February. During the harvest in February, entire families move to the
fincas, where Chatino boys and girls, women and men work as wage
laborers picking coffee. During the remainder of the year, these campesinos cultivate their own plots of land.

During the 1950s and 1960s, the Chatino community underwent
important economic changes. Until that time their main crops were
beans and corn for local consumption. In general, the Chatinos were
self-sufficient, and land was distributed equally among them. Communal ownership and production techniques dominant at that time
encouraged this equitable situation.[5] According to the testimonies of
Chatino elders,[6] no one person held a piece of land permanently, and
no one was the owner of any particular plot of land.

Until 1950, only a small portion of Chatino land was planted in
coffee. But during the 1950s, much of the land suitable for coffee production was brought under cultivation, in response to expansion by
established coffee growers and because of the entry of new coffee
growers to the region. By 1991, 9,367 individual farms were registered in Juquila (INEGI 1996: 437). Taking into consideration the fact
that initially there were 3,000 coffee growers in the organizations
registered under the Chatinos Unidos Union alone, and that, according to the author's calculations, almost 30 percent of the region's

---

[5] The Chatinos practiced slash-and-burn agriculture. A plot of land cleared by this
technique would be used for four consecutive years, after which it would lie fallow
for eight years so that its fertility could be regained. The same plot could be used over
and over again by following this cycle. But in order to apply this technique, farmers
had to have access to several plots so that some could be cultivated while other lay
fallow. As long as the Chatinos had access to open, unused communal lands, the system functioned well, and each family "owned" only that plot that they were currently
cultivating. In this way, no one person accumulated more land than they could easily
cultivate.
[6] In the indigenous communities, elders play a very important role in that they constitute a collegial body that advises on issues of local government.

farmers have not joined any association, one can assume that at least half of all farmers in the region today are directly involved in growing coffee. This increase is due principally to the growth in coffee demand and the rise in international prices for coffee, as well as in response to government intervention during the 1970s and early 1980s aimed at promoting the cultivation and marketing of coffee.

Several local factors also contributed to the expansion of coffee production. First, the Chatinos were familiar with the techniques of coffee cultivation because they had been working on coffee plantations since the end of the nineteenth century. Second, a group of mestizo businessmen who operated in the region and were looking to improve their market position encouraged the Chatinos to plant coffee. Because outsiders are not allowed to own communal land directly, these businessmen maneuvered to gain access to land by other routes; they provided Chatino farmers with the means to cultivate coffee—in the form of loans made on the condition that the crop would be sold exclusively to the lenders. In addition, newcomer mestizo farmers arrived in the Chatino region, and they took whatever steps necessary to become "citizens" of the Chatino community in order to gain the right to plant the land.[7] This practice has a long history; some of the oldest plantation families had used this strategy when they first arrived in the region to make their fortunes in coffee.

The cycle of coffee production is a lengthy one. Coffee bushes mature and produce their first harvestable beans four years after planting. And the plants do not reach top yield until year eight, after which they continue to produce fruit for another twenty to thirty years. Despite the Chatino practice of holding land communally, the requirement that coffee plants must be nurtured over a span of many years has led to coffee fields becoming, de facto, a farmer's permanent possession.

Thus land planted in coffee has been particularly susceptible to transformation into a form of privately held property that can be bought and sold, even though such transactions are technically illegal. The Chatinos circumvent the legal stricture against selling communal land by declaring that they do not, in fact, sell the land; they sell the coffee bushes that are planted on it and the value of the work they have invested as cultivators. This rationale has guided practice since the 1950s; the only restriction imposed on sales is that they may not be made to people from outside the Chatino region. That im-

---

[7] Some of the mestizos have risen to positions of significant social and political importance in the Chatino communities. A teacher in Panixtlahuaca and a priest in Teotepec and Yaitepec have both become owners of large farms (Greenberg 1981; Hernández Díaz 1987).

pediment has, to some degree, slowed the transformation of the indigenous lands into a commodity in the fullest sense of the word (Greenberg 1981: 138; Hernández Díaz 1987).

With the increase in coffee cultivation, the availability of land has decreased to the point that people are hard pressed to locate plots on which to grow corn. Because land has become increasingly scarce, individuals now try to retain plots permanently. This, in turn, has meant that the period during which a plot is left fallow has shortened or has disappeared altogether, with the result that the land's overall fertility and productivity have decreased dramatically. Without a doubt, this transformation in the Chatinos' pattern of land tenure has been a significant development for their community, and it has been caused primarily by the spread of coffee cultivation. Not only has the transformation affected areas planted in coffee; it has also made plots where corn and other crops are grown subject to de facto privatization.

Government Intervention in the Coffee Sector

Government intervention in coffee production in Oaxaca began in the nineteenth century. In 1875, Governor José Esperón signed a decree aimed at promoting production by exempting investors from paying taxes on money invested in coffee production. This especially benefited the large landholders, who began taking over communal lands belonging to the indigenous population (Bartra 1996). Later, in 1946, the federal government created the National Coffee Council (Consejo Nacional del Café), but its influence on the activities of Oaxaca's coffee growers was minimal. It was replaced by the Mexican Coffee Institute (INMECAFÉ), created by presidential decree in 1958. INMECAFÉ's mission was to regulate coffee prices, provide technical assistance, and conduct research aimed at improving production and controlling pest infestations. From the outset, it focused its efforts on regulating exports.

During the administration of President Luis Echeverría (1970–1976), government policy turned toward support for small coffee farmers, with the goal of improving their levels of production and standard of living. In addition to regulating prices, the policy aimed to organize growers into small cells, called Economic Units for Production and Marketing (UEPCs). By 1989, INMECAFÉ had organized about 80 percent of small coffee farmers (Hernández 1991: 17–48). In 1980, INMECAFÉ purchased 30 percent of the coffee produced in the Chatino region; according to local calculations, this share had increased substantially by 1989, with the remainder of the crop being sold—as it still is—to private buyers in the towns of Juquila and Nopala. These buyers are part of a wider network of coffee brokers that ends in Oaxaca City with the owners of the major coffee-processing plants, who are often also the large plantation owners.

The principal aims of the UEPCs were to distribute credit, deliver technical assistance, and organize the marketing process for IN-MECAFÉ. The UEPC cells were affiliated automatically with the National Peasants' Confederation, the rural corporatist organization controlled by the ruling Institutional Revolutionary Party (PRI). The influence of INMECAFÉ among the Chatino farmers was always limited because, even though it made short-term loans secured by the forthcoming harvest, these loans were available only at designated times. Furthermore, INMECAFÉ paid for the harvested crop only after it was sold on the international market. For that reason, although INMECAFÉ generally offered better prices than the local middlemen, the small farmers were often forced to sell to the latter, who gave them immediate credit and paid for the crop without a delay, albeit at lower prices.

As part of a new policy initiated during the administration of President Miguel de la Madrid (1982–1988) and carried out during the presidency of Carlos Salinas de Gortari (1988–1994), INMECAFÉ was disbanded in a process that began in 1989 and ended in 1993. Although the Chatino farmers had questioned the value of INMECAFÉ, today many of them are sorry that it is gone. According to a leader of Shalyuu-Kia, Panixtlahuaca:

> I think that it was a sad event for the coffee growers when INMECAFÉ disappeared because it had offered useful programs: those dealing with seedlings, greenhouses, rehabilitation and renovation of the coffee bushes, technical help with fertilizers and with pruning. These programs helped us improve production. When INMECAFÉ disappeared, we went through a serious crisis. And it got worse in the 1990s when the price of coffee went down and we couldn't even find buyers for our crop. When INMECAFÉ was operating, not only did they support us with agricultural programs, they also helped us with marketing our crop (author interview, May 1996).

The farmers' economic situation worsened with the international crisis in coffee prices. With the suspension in 1989 of the International Coffee Agreement, the quota system, in which fifty producer countries and twenty-four consumer countries had participated, ended. The price of coffee fell from an average of U.S.$1.16 per pound to 68 cents in 1990 (Arango Londoño 1994: 265, 281). As a consequence, the amount of land in Oaxaca dedicated to coffee cultivation dropped from 189,300 hectares in 1991 to 180,374 hectares in 1995. This decline is even more notable when one considers that the area actually harvested declined from 184,700 hectares in 1991 to only 151,067 in 1995 (INEGI 1996).

With INMECAFÉ's withdrawal and the liberalization of the coffee market, the coffee farmers were at the mercy of the laws of supply and demand and under the sway of middlemen, known as *coyotes*, who honed their exploitative tactics, as the farmers themselves recount:

> There are coyotes who pay in advance; for example, the people right now are saying: "I don't have any money left. I'm going to go to those men who buy my coffee to see if I can get a loan, to see if they will give me some sugar or maybe some corn." And the coyotes given them corn, and they give them sugar, and they give them enough beans to survive; but then at harvest time, when it is time to harvest the coffee crop, then they come asking for payment.... Then they say, "Pay me with interest" ... and some charge as much as 10 percent, and others charge 15 and even 20 percent in monthly interest (author interview with a coffee grower, Panixtlahuaca, January 1997).

This has happened in the Chatino region just as it has happened elsewhere. Faced with these circumstances, the growers have experimented with new ways of organizing, particularly in associations that are independent of the government.

Although the federal government reduced its presence in the coffee sector with the dismantling of INMECAFÉ, it did not go away entirely. A new organization was created, the Mexican Coffee Council, in which participated the Ministries of Agriculture,[8] Social Development (SEDESOL), Finance (SHCP), and Commerce and Industrial Development (SECOFI), along with governors of the coffee-producing states and representatives of the key producer organizations. In Oaxaca, a State Coffee Council was formed, presided over by the governor, who has the power to appoint the council's executive director. Representatives from producer organizations, industrial and export associations, and the state and federal government agencies involved in the coffee sector also participated. With the help of the

---

[8] The Mexican Ministry of Agriculture was known as the Secretaría de Agricultura y Recursos Hidráulicos (Ministry of Agriculture and Water Resources, or SARH) until the end of the Salinas de Gortari administration in 1994. Under Salinas's successor, President Ernesto Zedillo, the ministry was renamed the Secretaría de Agricultura, Ganadería y Desarrollo Rural (Ministry of Agriculture, Livestock, and Rural Development, or SAGAR).

National Indigenous Institute (INI), the State Coffee Council, in turn, has promoted the creation of Regional Coffee Councils, which comprise community-level assemblies of coffee growers. For example, in the Chatino region, fifty-six community assemblies participate in the Regional Council, and many of them are a continuation of the UEPC cells established years ago by INMECAFÉ.

In 1990, in response to demands from producer organizations, the government used funds from the National Solidarity Program (PRONASOL) and administered by INI to assist small farmers by providing a specific amount of money for each hectare under coffee cultivation, up to a maximum of 5 hectares. The program continued until 1994. Federal government policy toward the coffee growers changed with the new administration of President Ernesto Zedillo (1994–2000), however, and by the 1995–1996 harvest, subsidies had been suspended and the producers were forced to seek out new lenders. As will be shown later, the loans they negotiated were made in dollars, causing a series of problems that led to delays in the repayment of the loans. The policy shift reflected proposals made by the two government agencies that have had the greatest influence over the design of federal policies for the coffee sector: the Ministry of Agriculture and the Ministry of Social Development. Implementation of these policies in the Chatino region has been the responsibility of the local INI offices, headquartered in Juquila, and the local SAGAR offices, headquartered in Nopala. The federal government has left it up to the officials in these agencies to encourage the organization of agricultural producers in the region.

Coffee Producer Organizations in the Chatino Region

In Oaxaca, state government policy toward coffee growers took an interesting twist during the administration of Governor Heladio Ramírez López (1986–1992). Staying one step ahead of national-level changes, the state government tried to fill the vacuum left by the dismantling of INMECAFÉ. On February 5, 1990, it passed a law to support the promotion and expansion of coffee agriculture in the state.[9] Fausto Cantú Peña, one of the principal proponents of INMECAFÉ, acted as the governor's adviser on this matter. As a prelude to the new policy, the governor pushed for the unionization of small farmers; part of his administration's plan included the formation of second- and third-level campesino organizations corresponding to

---

[9] The law was published in the official government newspaper on April 4, 1990.

the various production sectors, in order to facilitate the implementation of production projects (Aranda 1992: 91, 101).

As a result, three coffee producer organizations operate today in the Chatino region: Kyat-ñuu, Chatinna, and Shalyuu-Kia. These, in turn, form part of the Chatinos Union, which includes campesinos residing in the municipalities of San Juan Quiahije, Santiago Yaitepec, San Juan Lachao, Santos Reyes Nopala, Santa Catarina Juquila, San Miguel Panixtlahuaca, and Santa María Temaxcaltepec. Two other associations are also members of Chatinos Unidos: Yucuu-café, which comprises mostly Mixtec and mestizo growers in the municipality of San Pedro Tututepec, and the Organization of Chatino Women (ORMICH), with its headquarters in the municipal seat of Juquila.

Both Kyat-ñuu and Chatinna were sponsored by the state government since their inception in the mid–1980s. Kyat-ñuu was founded on October 29, 1986, as a Unión de Comunidades (association of community assemblies). Shalyuu-Kia has its antecedents in the organizing work of Tomás Cruz Lorenzo, an indigenous leader in the region who had fought to defend the interests of communities in the municipality of Quiahije against logging companies. When Cruz Lorenzo was assassinated in 1990, his supporters regrouped Shalyuu-Kia with the support of the INI.

These producer organizations began to gain importance after 1990, when they were required to take part in activities orchestrated by the federal government as part of PRONASOL. As a prerequisite for obtaining economic aid under this program, the government required that campesinos be formally organized. Farmers could not receive benefits—through the Regional Solidarity Funds, or FRS, program, for example—unless they joined a Solidarity Committee at the community level and were affiliated with broader organizations. The INI oversaw the implementation of this strategy, which began with pilot programs in Puebla, Oaxaca, Guerrero, and Chiapas and later spread throughout Mexico.

Even though the three producer organizations examined in this chapter had different origins, at the urging of INI officials and for administrative reasons, all ultimately adopted the same organizational structure, which begins at the community level with assemblies in which all affiliated producers participate. Each assembly selects four delegates, to represent the community's coffee growers, cattle ranchers, chicken farmers, and basic-food producers, respectively. One of these four delegates is chosen to represent the assembly in the Chatinos Unidos Union. Within each organization, the delegates from all communities select an administrative council, consisting of a president, secretary, treasurer, and their alternates, and an oversight council, also formed by a president, a secretary, and their alternates.

Eight communities are members of Kyat-ñuu. Four are municipal seats: Santa María Temaxcaltepec, San Juan Lachao Nuevo, San Gabriel Mixtepec, and Santos Reyes Nopala; the other four are submunicipal seats of Nopala: Santa María Magdalena Tiltepec, Santiago Cuixtla, Cerro del Aire, and Santa Lucía Teotepec. Thus Kyat-ñuu's board of directors consists of thirty-two people, four from each of the eight member communities. The key seats on the board go to individuals who reside in Nopala. Even though the representatives justify those appointments by arguing that it is easier to conduct business with people who live locally, this arrangement has raised concern among growers from other towns, who believe that the appointments are motivated by political favoritism.

Shalyuu-Kia consists of three municipal seats: Panixtlahuaca, Quiahije, and Yaitepec, as well as three submunicipal seats of Juquila: San Francisco Ixpantepec, Santa María Amialtepec, and Santa María Yolotepec. Chatinna comprises the growers in the municipal seat of Juquila and in one of its submunicipal seats.

Each board of directors is appointed for a period of three years. As of 1997, the Kyat-ñuu was in its fourth administration. It is the most stable of the three organizations, something that is reflected in the growth of its membership and the infrastructure projects that it has carried out, which include a coffee-processing plant; a grocery store; and its own programs for purchasing pesticides. The principal objective of the directors of Kyat-ñuu is to help acquaint its members with the government programs available to its member communities. As one of the directors pointed out:

> We've noticed that the communities themselves often do not hear about the government programs or understand how they must organize in order to get help in resolving the problems they are facing. Thanks to the support of some of our delegates, we have an organization that is a little more cohesive.... And in some ways this has made advances possible, but I also believe that we should work to improve the organization, because if we do not take care of this aspect of things, I think it could all fall apart at any moment (author interview with a delegate from Kyat-ñuu, Nopala, December 1996).

This statement shows that both the membership and the directors of the organizations believe that their purpose is to encourage participation in programs run by the government and that their stability is basically due to government support. Even though it is true that a primary reason the Chatinos around Nopala affiliated with Kyat-ñuu was to seek improved marketing opportunities for their coffee crop, it is also true that, under the circumstances in which they found themselves, they could not have survived without assistance from the outside—in this case, help from the state government and later from the federal government. But the most important catalyst for joining was the crisis in coffee prices during the early 1990s, as one of the growers explains:

> At that time, we realized the need to seek outside help or programs in order to maintain or sustain our families.... We are talking about the 1990s, when coffee prices were very depressed, and we really needed those programs to keep going. I believe that if it weren't for those programs, we wouldn't be growing coffee right now (author interview with a member of the board of directors, Kyat-ñuu, Nopala, December 1996).

According to the Chatino growers, since the disappearance of INMECAFÉ, the farmers have received government assistance only through the State Coffee Council, which in reality has played a limited role. Improving production and marketing has been the responsibility principally of the producers themselves.

The Kyat-ñuu has helped the Chatino coffee growers expand their activities and move into areas that most of them could not have entered on their own. With the backing of the membership, they have gotten new assistance—for example, from Regional Solidarity Funds and the Oaxaca state government. With that money, the Kyat-ñuu leadership built a dry-processing plant. The labor was provided by the members of the organization through a system of cooperative and collective work known in Oaxaca as *tequio*. The result, however, has not always been what was hoped for. For example, the processing plant was not used until 1996, three years after construction was complete. According to a member of the board of directors:

> We hadn't thought about starting up the coffee processing facility and its machinery ourselves; but, with the support of the delegates, we decided to get it up and running. In some ways, we have concerned ourselves with marketing more than anything else because, like it or not, marketing is the most difficult problem we face. The market is uncertain, unstable. For the same reason, we took a risk to find whoever pays the most for the coffee and who gives us the best guarantees (author interview, Kyat-ñuu, January 1997).

After operating for two years, the processing plant was put up for sale because it was not as profitable as was hoped and may even have lost money. In marketing, by contrast, Kyat-ñuu has achieved significant success because, in addition to financial gains, it has also managed to secure the support of a large number of coffee growers. Its marketing accomplishments are due to a specific strategy. First, it acquired Regional Solidarity Funds monies to purchase a truck so that members could transport their crop to the warehouses cheaply. It then purchased a second truck with funds of its own saved from the profits earned from the sale of coffee stored at the warehouse.[10] In the eyes of the growers, the organization had taken a great step forward because it had freed them from one part of the chain of intermediaries and thereby increased their profit margin:

> Transportation from here to, say, Oaxaca City would cost us 1,400 pesos. Figuring that, with the truck we just bought, a 12–ton truck, transport only costs $550, we are saving almost $850 (author interview with a coffee grower in Nopala, December 1996).

As Kyat-ñuu has been solidifying its organization, its members have also been expanding their boundaries both commercially and politically. For example, today the organization sells directly to the large coffee merchants. Unionized producers also sell their crop together as a bloc to private export firms such as Cafetalera San Francisco, which is an offshoot of Agroindustrias Unidas de México (formerly Tiasa), and Becafisa which in Oaxaca is associated with Grupo Audelo.[11] Nevertheless, many more growers continue signing over all or part of their crop to brokers at less than optimal prices because of their need to settle outstanding debts. The middlemen still monopolize the purchase of most of the region's coffee output. But at least now the Kyat-ñuu sells much of its produce directly to the exporters, and it is making an attempt to export directly to the international market.

In the past, a long chain of middlemen lay between the small farmers and the exporter or the export company. The new arrangement benefits both the producer and the exporter. The large exporters

---

[10] During the 1995–1996 harvest, Kyat-ñuu purchased between 70 and 80 percent of the coffee produced by the small farmers in the area around Nopala, and from that it earned 1,400,000 new pesos. $1,100,000 was reimbursed to the producers to equalize prices, following the same system that INMECAFÉ had employed. The remainder was used to purchase a truck.

[11] According to rough figures provided by an industrialist in the Oaxaca coffee business, Becafisa exported almost 20 percent of the coffee harvested in Oaxaca during 1996, while Agroindustrias Unidas de México bought almost 70 percent. The remaining 10 percent was exported by independent organizations such as CEPCO, UCI "Cien Años," UCIRI, and UCIZONI.

now have more direct control over the producers and enjoy some economic advantages. By avoiding the chain of intermediaries, exporters reduce their costs and the risks that arise when the coffee crop must pass through the hands of local and regional merchants. Now that the output reaches them directly, the exporters no longer have to deal with and pay a series of middlemen.

Although it is true that the Kyat-ñuu was founded and operates as an organization linked to the government and to the party in power (the director of Kyat-ñuu and of Chatinos Unidos is currently the local PRI deputy for the Coast region),[12] it is also true that the organization tries to follow a policy that is more or less independent and to focus its activities on resolving economic problems the growers face in marketing the coffee crop.

Together with the other producer organizations, Kyat-ñuu has negotiated for resources with the banks and government agencies. Thus, for example, the members actively participate in meetings of the State Coffee Council. They also maintain commercial and political ties, not only with the organizations affiliated with the government, but also with independent organizations that have been characterized by their policy of working apart from government agencies. They have obtained loans from CEPCO to finance their purchasing of coffee, and from other sources such as the Union of Organizations from the Sierra Juárez of Oaxaca (UNOSJO), which lent machinery for construction of a gas station.

The Kyat-ñuu is one of the most successful organizations in the area supervised by the Indigenous Coordinating Center (CCI) headquartered in Juquila. In September 1996, Kyat-ñuu opened a grocery store, and in 1995 it began construction of a gas station which opened for business in 1997. Financing for these works came primarily from federal government programs, but the organization raised some of the project funding as well.

The board of directors has emphasized that the organization includes both coffee growers and other community members, so that the people affiliated with the organization are "whoever lives in the communities served by the association." Despite these claims, however, the active members are primarily coffee farmers, and the intention of the board of directors and INI officials is to support the growers in their capacity as members of these communities. With this strategy, they hope to increase the overall membership and extend their clientelist control in the community. The latter is an especially important goal because, for bureaucratic reasons, the performance of

---

[12] Fausto Mijangos, the director of Chatinos Unidos, was a proxy for the state-level deputy from the Coast region, who ran for a seat as a federal representative.

the INI officials is measured by the number of people they can report as having benefited from their programs. The board of directors acknowledges that the organization is driven by the government agencies:

> Well, everything has come from the programs, which are the result of the national-level PRONASOL project. That's where the support for all different kinds of production sectors originated.... It was through those regional funds that the Chatinos Unidos Union was formed, and that is where we have been trying to take part in all the projects that they provide, because we have seen that they benefit the growers more than anyone else (author interview with Fausto Mijangos, Kyat-ñuu, Nopala, May 1996).

Nevertheless, not all growers see the relationship in such a positive light. In Quiahije, the members have begun to question the dependence on government agencies and have tried to form a splinter group, encouraged by people with ties to ecclesiastical activists working in the region covered by Shalyuu-Kia. Similarly, the growers in San Juan Lachao have criticized the marketing strategy that Kyat-ñuu followed during the 1996–1997 season. Because of fluctuations in the price of coffee—the price was 506 new pesos per hundred pounds in December 1996 and $1,200 per hundred pounds in April 1997—the organization was forced to pay a lower price to its members than other growers got by selling to brokers. Members complained, and they insist that their affiliation with Kyat-ñuu has hurt rather than helped them. This situation was discussed in an assembly at which most farmers accepted the price set by the organization, and some recalled that in the past, thanks to being organized, they had been able to get better prices, for which reason they should now support their organization's administrative council.

According to the directors of the organizations in the Chatino region, all agricultural producers who reside in the region are organization members. Regarding Kyat-ñuu, for example, in theory, all of the 2,500–plus growers residing in the area participate. In reality, only those who receive funds from government programs are beneficiaries; and in this case, the funds have been channeled preferentially to the coffee growers. Thus in 1994, those formally affiliated with the Chatinos Unidos Union numbered 2,872, but by 1996 the membership had declined to 1,503, even though the members of the Yucuu-café organization were included in the second count but not in the first.

The success of the Chatinos Unidos Union in marketing coffee encouraged coffee growers who were members to participate in other projects, such as the purchase of cattle, manufacture of bricks and roofing materials, flower cultivation, home repair, bread making, and manufacture of products made from ixtle, among other things. All these production projects have received government financing through programs run by the Ministry of Social Development. Even though these projects have not all been as successful as the earlier programs—or prompted the same high level of membership involvement—they continue to achieve high loan-repayment rates in comparison to the performance of similar groups receiving monies through Regional Solidarity Funds.[13]

Although INI officials take pains to point out that the organizations are made up of *communities*, in reality they consist of a given number of coffee farmers, basically those who have one hectare or more under coffee cultivation. The smallest producers, those with less than a hectare of land, do not receive assistance, and, obviously, the large landholders are not members.

Producer Organizations and Collective Loans

Between 1990 and 1994, when international coffee prices were in decline, the federal government gave subsidies to small farmers through the Support Program for Coffee Growers (Programa de Apoyo a los Productores de Café), funds that producers in the Chatino region pledged to repay in full to the government through their organizations. The Chatinos' repayment program was one of the most efficient, according to an ex-director of INI's Indigenous Coordinating Center in Juquila. In some communities, producers repaid 100 percent of the funds. The directors of Chatinos Unidos claim that this commitment to repay the loans came from the producers themselves, who in some cases even had to sell property in order to raise the money. However, the arrangement was a form of interest-free loans, given that producers returned only the amount received, without interest.

Moreover, the recovered funds remained under the control of the organizations and were administered by their directors. According to these directors, the money was at first reinvested, under an agreement reached with INI officials, by lending it at a monthly interest rate of 1.5 percent. In this way, the organizations built up a fund of 9 million new pesos. Given the substantial size of the fund, the INI officials suggested that the money should be administered so that it

---

[13] An internal INI document written in 1997 notes that Chatinos Unidos was among the five organizations in Oaxaca with the best loan repayment record.

could be better managed and, moreover, so that it could be handled in a manner congruent with the collectivist practices of Chatino indigenous culture. Legal entities—community chests—were created to manage the accumulated capital. From the perspective of the INI officials, this arrangement fit well within the communal culture of the region. The money came to be handled by an administrative council whose members, in theory, were subordinates of the growers' organizations, but who, in fact, operated independently.

According to the directors and rank and file of the producer organizations, the community chests were created at their initiative. But this development was, in fact, part of a wider government program. In 1994, after the federal government had operated the Support Program for Coffee Growers for four years, it transferred the program's funding and responsibilities to the communities through their community chests. The latter were reconfigured as civil associations so that they would be able to increase their net worth and to channel support to coffee producers more easily. Seven community chests were created in the Chatino region, reportedly established with the capital that each producer had contributed as repayment for government assistance received. Thus the farmers became shareholders in the community chests and saw the community chests' assets as their own (see table 4.1).

After the creation of the community chests, the directors of the producer organizations proposed ways to use these funds to benefit community members who were not coffee producers. For example, a loan program for basic goods was implemented to help farmers during the planting season for corn and beans. Another program loaned money for purchases of herbicides, fertilizers, and fumigation equipment, and recouped the money at harvest time or when the peasants received support from PROCAMPO.[14] Nevertheless, the community chests were also a source of confusion and tension among the growers. At the outset, both the INI officials and the boards of directors believed that the community chests were dependent on the organizations. But the chests' administrative councils acted autonomously of the organizations. This situation generated conflicts between the organizations' directors and the chest administrative councils because no one was ready to cede their control over the management of the capital. With the transference of the resources, INI formally stopped intervening in matters relating to loans for coffee production.

---

[14] PROCAMPO is a federal government assistance program to producers of basic agricultural goods. It provides a set amount of money per hectare.

TABLE 4.1
COMMUNITY CHESTS IN THE CHATINO REGION

Community Chest	Number of Communities[1]	Share-holders	Assets[2] (new pesos)
LOS TRES REYES Stos. Reyes Nopala Kyat-ñuu	10	475	681,272.50
SANTA ANA TUTUTEPEC Santa Ana Tututepec Yucuu-café	4	260	540,817.31
KTCHE-TZI San Marcos Zacatepec Chatinna	4	276	379,822.18
KINÑOT I KENSHI Santiago Yaitepec Shalyuu-kia	1	333	462,665.00
SAN JUAN San Juan Lachao Kyat-ñuu	8	448	725,812.40
SANTA CATARINA JUQUILA Chatinna	12	541	782,284.00
UNIFICACIÓN Y PROGRESO El Camalote Juquila Chatinna	11	443	550,245.00
TOTAL	50	2,776	4,122,918.39

Source: Archives of the Indigenous Coordinating Central in Juquila.
[1] Communities that received direct INI–Grupo Operativo Regional transfers are not included.
[2] Resources transferred through the INI, without factoring in debts owned.

During the 1995–1996 harvest, the State Coffee Council, through BANCOMEXT and BANRURAL, was the entity that managed loans for producers. Each producer could receive a loan in dollars equivalent to 1000 pesos per hectare up to 5 hectares. In order to obtain this funding, a loan guaranty fund had to be put together to which the growers, the INI, the state government, and FIDECAFE would each contribute. It was agreed that once a grower had liquidated his debt, he would be reimbursed for the part he had contributed to the guaranty fund and for the part provided by the INI. In most cases, the grower's contribution was made with money from the community chests and the Regional Solidarity Funds program. Unfortunately for the growers, their debt increased with the peso devaluation. Even though the growers acknowledged that they owed 1,000 pesos per hectare and many repaid the loan, BANCOMEXT nevertheless charged the remaining debt against the loan guaranty fund.

The coffee growers have now lost faith because they feel they have been tricked. The leaders of the Chatinos Unidos say that it has become very difficult to convince the farmers that their loan guaranty fund had vanished. That situation has weakened the organizations and also undermined the "culture of repayment" that previously existed among the Chatinos.

From Kyat-ñuu to Chatinos Unidos

The organizing efforts of producer organizations in the Chatino region received an extra stimulus from the drop in coffee prices, because growers could only count on the loans they so desperately needed if they were affiliated with an organization that would back them. This situation led the INI officials to encourage the formation of the Chatinos Unidos Union, with Kyat-ñuu at its head. Chatinos Unidos was created as a legal entity on August 26, 1994. The leaders of Kyat-ñuu and Chatinos Unidos clearly adhered to the opinion that it was officials in government agencies who were responsible for organizing the coffee growers in this structure:

> The government official who led us, who prepared us to organize as growers, and who taught us how to work together was an engineer, Abel Bernal Domínguez, the director of the Indigenous Coordinating Center in Juquila. He had the idea of combining the organizations and our support because, despite having been well taught and prepared by the Center, if the organizations had not accepted the idea, well, it never would have gotten off the ground. But it did. There was good coordination, and that is why right now we are constituted as a union and we have gotten as far as we have (author interview with Fausto Mijangos, Juquila, 1996).

The proposal was not well received by all growers. The rank and file in Kyat-ñuu protested, claiming that the successes of their organization will now be seen as victories for Chatinos Unidos and that any goods and resources acquired by them will be considered property of the whole union. The members of Kyat-ñuu complain that this has already occurred with the coffee-processing plant and the gas station. For their part, the members of Chatinna and of Shalyuu-Kia feel that their ability to make decisions on actions taken by Chatinos Unidos has been curtailed.

In the Chatinos Unidos Union, those with the most decision-making power are members of the Kyat-ñuu board of directors. This is evident in the implicit understanding that the president or a board member of that organization always holds the Chatino Unidos presidency.

INI officials have been influential in both the formation of Chatinos Unidos and in its operation. The Ministry of Agriculture (SAGAR), the other major government agency active in the region, also took part in creating the union and has had some influence over its administrative council (one of whose members is married to a SAGAR official residing in Nopala). But the INI officials have definitely emerged as the dominant force in directing the activities of both Kyat-ñuu (an organization in which SAGAR officials played an important developmental role) and Chatinos Unidos. This has occasioned a good deal of friction between the officials of the two agencies. The Ministry people insist that the INI has tried, through its involvement in the creation of Chatinos Unidos, to inflate the importance of its work, presenting the Kyat-ñuu's achievements as their own.

The INI's influence is easily visible in the work of a group of professionals from Juquila who were hired by Chatinos Unidos as a technical support team. This team—an administrator, assistants, secretaries, two agricultural engineers, and a lawyer—decides what activities the union will carry out, and its office functions as part of the INI's Indigenous Coordinating Center in Juquila. Under certain circumstances, the directors of the Union are forced to take a secondary role in decision making, as a key leader of Kyat-ñuu and Chatinos Unidos explained:

> We, the directorate, live so far away from Juquila,[15] which
> is the headquarters of Chatinos Unidos, that we are forced
> to appoint an attorney as proxy, and this attorney is
> housed in the offices [of the INI], where he can take part in
> decision making on different issues that we are required to
> address in our role as the board of directors (author inter-
> view with Fausto Mijangos, Nopala, January 1997).

---

[15] The leaders of Kyat-ñuu reside in Nopala, and it takes them six hours by bus to reach Juquila.

It is assumed that all the affiliated organizations should participate in the monthly meetings of Chatinos Unidos, but only a small portion of the delegates actually attend. Under the best of circumstances, the president and one or two delegates from each association are present. Overall, the meetings are attended mostly by delegates from Kyat-ñuu, the members of the technical support team, and officials of the CCI. Thus it is reasonable to say that the real decision makers in the Chatinos Unidos Union are the leaders of Kyat-ñuu and the INI officials. The delegates from Chatinna and Shalyuu-Kia attend primarily when they know in advance that the discussions will cover the distribution of monetary resources (loans or subsidies) that might eventually benefit their membership.

The Culture of the Chatino Coffee Farmers

The members of these producer organizations are mostly Chatino-speaking Indians (only 30 percent are mestizo, or "Spanish-ized," as one local Kyat-ñuu leader described it). Coffee cultivation has led to important changes in Chatino culture. Perhaps the most important has been the transformation of concepts regarding land ownership. Once all the available area that was appropriate for coffee was put under cultivation, individual plots—which represent a significant investment of a farmer's time and money—increasingly came to be considered an individual's permanent holding. This weakened the concept of land as a collective good, as property of the community. Yet this has not undermined the Chatinos' ability to defend their unique cultural traditions.

Language plays an important role in the preservation of cultural diversity. In the Chatino region, as well as in other regions of Oaxaca where indigenous campesino communities predominate, local issues are discussed in assemblies in the native language. In several of the communities discussed in this chapter, Chatino is the language spoken during assemblies. In places such as Tiltepec, Teotepec, Cerro del Aire, or Temaxcaltepec, representatives to regional producer organizations should be fluent in the language that the majority of the producers speak. Yet even though the small farmers affiliated with the producer organizations speak Chatino, their delegates, in general, are monolingual Spanish speakers. The fact that almost all the delegates are Spanish speakers becomes apparent during the monthly meetings of Chatinos Unidos, which are conducted solely in that language. In community assemblies, in contrast, people speak Chatino and a Spanish-speaking interpreter translates for any government official who wants to participate in the meeting.

Even though ethnic difference is a fact, it was not a motivating factor in the founding of the producer organizations. The farmers organized as producers, not as Indians or Chatinos. Ethnicity and the participation of women have only recently been added as discussion topics in assemblies, and their inclusion owes much to prompting by the INI. However, the ethnicity issue has quickly gained salience, and directors of the organizations in Chatinos Unidos—who may or may not identify themselves as Chatinos—are quick to make reference to the close ties between their organizations and the region's culture:

> Like it or not, we are descended from fathers and grandfa-
> thers who were Chatinos. Even though we don't speak
> Chatino fluently, we consider ourselves Chatinos and have
> no reason to be ashamed of that fact (author interview with
> Fausto Mijangos, president of Kyat-ñuu).

Although there are cultural differences between the leadership and the rank and file, there is a commensurate concern to smooth over any distinctions, to the point that the organizations are demanding cultural reparations based on their self-identity as ethnically differentiated entities. In the case of Kyat-ñuu, these demands are increasingly couched in terms of reparations of an ethnic nature, and the organization insists on strengthening its cultural traditions. The indigenous name the members selected for their organization clearly carries important symbolic meaning which nurtures and orients a sense of community and endows Kyat-ñuu's agricultural and service projects with an image that is uniquely the community's own. Thus, for example, the members of Kyat-ñuu have developed their own techniques for planting—*cero labranza* (zero labor) or *labranza de conservación* (conservation work)—and these planting methods are associated with the protection of their lands and their indigenous culture. This discourse contributes to the revitalization of the indigenous values and ethnic identity of campesino producers in the Chatino region.

This is a noteworthy development because the Chatinos originally organized as coffee producers in order to qualify for government benefits. Yet today they are also making demands based on self-identity as part of a distinct ethnic community.

Conclusion

As noted at the beginning of this chapter, campesinos who are not members of one of Oaxaca's independent organizations have undertaken relatively impressive organizing efforts, and these efforts have not always been inspired by corporatist motives. In the case of Kyat-ñuu, for example, discussions among farmers over losses resulting from the leaders' marketing strategy is an example of the producers' determination to defend their association. Today, many of them are affiliated with Kyat-ñuu solely at their own, individual initiative because they recognize the benefits of being organized.

The case of the producer organizations that make up the Chatinos Unidos Union reveals a relationship of constant negotiation that can provoke conflict among the different actors involved in the bargaining. The government agencies do not necessarily act uniformly. For example, the policies of the INI tend to privilege the growers' associations even though officially its mission is to defend indigenous culture, which, in this case, would be better served if the INI's actions were focused on the community level. In contrast, this appears to be the strategy of the Ministry of Agriculture, whose official assignment does not include the defense of local culture but whose actions are, nevertheless, directed at the community level because the issues the agency must address are often negotiated in local assemblies. Consequently, INI officials must work closely with the leaders of the producer organizations, while SAGAR works primarily with local authorities such as the municipal government and ejidal officials.

In carrying out their mission, INI officials have taken advantage of the strong community-level solidarities that already exist in the region. These communities, however, lacked a strong background in administration of monetary resources. Even though some of the coffee growers had worked with INMECAFÉ, they did not have any direct experience in managing their own funds, nor in working with government agencies in a way that would allow them, through negotiation, to increase the resources they received from government programs. Only recently have they begun to present proposals for their own agricultural projects. These are still relatively modest initiatives because the proposals can be carried out only with the help of the INI officials; in some cases, they have actually been designed by those officials.

Although it is true that the coffee producer organizations in the Chatino region have emerged thanks to external support, it is not only organizations created by INI that have received outside help. In fact, several so-called independent organizations were founded with backing from outsiders. For example, proponents of liberation theology within the Catholic Church, who define their ministry as action on behalf of the poor, assisted both UCIRI and the Union of Indigenous Communities "One Hundred Years of Solitude" (UCI "Cien Años"). In the case of UCIRI, the participation of the clergy has been highly significant; a priest serves as its president. The principal adviser to the Union of Indigenous Communities of the Northern Isthmus (UCIZONI) is a former director of the INI's Indigenous Coordinating Center in that region. And CEPCO has been advised by a group of professionals and intellectuals who had previously worked together in a nongovernmental organization based in the capital city of Oaxaca.

Of the three coffee growers' organizations in the Chatino region, two lack formal experience in negotiation, implementation of projects, or administration and financing on their own behalf, and for these reasons they continue operating in the shadow of government agencies. This has caused tensions among the growers themselves (for example, in Quiahije), between the growers and the leaders of the organizations, among the organizations themselves, and between the organizations and the government agencies.

As far as the management of loans is concerned, even though the community chests were funded thanks to the growers' efforts to keep their loan payments current, this practice did not increase their capital because, in the end, the repaid funds belonged to the government, not to the Chatinos. Moreover, the whole scheme was not an idea developed by the Chatinos, and the program's design and rules were imposed on the growers by the government agencies.

In regard to the benefits the growers received from other government-sponsored projects, the true number of beneficiaries is smaller than bureaucrats report. They leave out an important sector of the campesinos: those with the fewest resources. The majority of the campesinos who receive aid are those who are the "least poor of the poor." This author estimates that more than half of the small farmers have not participated in the government-sponsored programs.

Despite conflict and tension, the campesinos in the Chatino region who initially organized at the urging of government officials have now developed, albeit inconsistently, programs that reinforce participatory practices. As limited as this participation may be, it should not be understood merely as a product of government-controlled corporatist organizing. In the cases analyzed here, even though campesino organizing was promoted from the top, the activities carried out by the coffee growers were the result of a continuous process of negotiation in which decisions were frequently taken and defended by the grassroots.

References

Aranda, Josefina. 1992. "Camino andado, retos y propuestas: la Coordinadora Estatal de Productores de Café de Oaxaca," *Cuadernos del Sur* 2 (1): 89–112.

Arango Londoño, Gilberto. 1994. "Por los senderos del café." Bogotá: Fondo Cultural Cafetero.

Bartra, Armando. 1996. *El México bárbaro. Plantaciones y monterías del sureste durante el Porfiriato.* Mexico: El Atajo.

Greenberg, James B. 1981. *Religión y economía de los Chatinos.* Mexico City: Instituto Nacional Indigenista.

Hernández, Luis. 1991. "Nadando con los tiburones: la experiencia de la Coordinadora Nacional de Organizaciones Cafetaleras." In *Cafetaleros: la construcción de la autonomía,* edited by Gabriela Ejea and Luis Hernández. Cuadernos de Desarrollo de Base, no. 3. Mexico City: Coordinadora Nacional de Organizaciones Cafetaleras.

Hernández Díaz, Jorge. 1987. *El café amargo. Diferenciación y cambio social entre los Chatinos.* Mexico: Instituto de Investigaciones Sociológicos, Universidad Autónoma "Benito Juárez" de Oaxaca.

———. 1995. "La Unión de Comunidades Indígenas de la Región del Istmo: viejas identidades sociales, nuevos references culturales y políticos," *Cuadernos del Sur* 8–9.

INEGI (Instituto Nacional de Estadística, Geografía e Informática). 1996. *Anuario estadístico del estado de Oaxaca.* Mexico City: INEGI/Gobierno del Estado de Oaxaca.

Martínez Morales, Aurora Cristina. 1997. *El proceso cafetalero mexicano.* Mexico City: Universidad Nacional Autónoma de México.

Moguel, Julio, and Josefina Aranda. 1992. "Los nuevos caminos en la construcción de la autonomía: la experiencia de la Coordinadora Estatal de Productores de Café de Oaxaca." In *Autonomía y nuevos sujetos del desarrollo rural,* edited by Julio Moguel, Carlota Botey, and Luis Hernández. Mexico City: Siglo Veintiuno.

Moguel, Julio, Carlota Botey, and Luis Hernández, eds. 1992. *Autonomía y nuevos sujetos del desarrollo rural.* Mexico City: Siglo Veintiuno.

Nolasco, Margarita. 1985. *Café y sociedad en México.* Mexico City: Centro de Ecodesarrollo.

Piñón Jiménez, Gonzalo. 1995. "Understanding Rural Development: A Case Study of Grassroots Coffee Organizations in the Isthmus Region of Oaxaca, Mexico." Ph.D. dissertation, Tulane University.

Rojas, Basilio. 1964. *El café.* Mexico: Instituto Mexicano del Café.

Romero, Matías. 1886. *El estado de Oaxaca.* Barcelona: Tipo-Litografía de Espasa.

SECOFI (Secretaría de Comercio y Fomento Industrial). 1997. Página informativa, *El Sur,* March 7.

Vazques y de los Santos, Elena, and Yanga Villagómez Velázquez. 1993. "La UCIRI, el café orgánico y la experiencia de un proyecto campesino autogestivo en la producción," *Cuadernos del Sur* 5 (2): 121–37.

5

The Building Blocks of Cooperation: Insights from Baja California

Jorge Mario Soto Romero

The reputation of rural co-ops in Mexico is not especially good these days. Governments as well as voluntary and religious organizations have promoted production cooperatives, credit associations, purchasing unions, and other similar groups—hereinafter referred to as co-ops—expecting to generate economic growth, improve equity, and empower the poor. The results, however, have often been disappointing. Inefficiency, corruption, entrenched leadership, and political manipulation have plagued many co-ops, causing members to disengage and leave. Moreover, recent reforms to the agrarian laws and the weakening of traditional patronage structures make it easier for producers to abandon co-ops. Today many people think of co-ops as anachronistic organizations, poorly suited, if at all, for the challenges and opportunities facing Mexico's rural sector.

The cooperative experience is diverse enough to qualify this pessimism. Many co-ops in Mexico and abroad certainly meet the expectations of their members (see Fox 1992; Tendler 1988; Attwood and Baviskar 1987; Wells 1982). In fact, some of them have succeeded in important ways despite having traits usually associated with failure, such as corruption and lack of democracy (Tendler 1988). Success or

The author thanks Richard Snyder for his invitation to participate in this volume and for his numerous comments on earlier drafts. Lisa Peattie, Alice Amsden, and Michael Piore provided valuable advice during the research, and Clemente Ruiz Durán and Alejandro Mungaray were supportive throughout this undertaking. Most of all, the author thanks the fishermen and farmers whose experience is presented here. All the opinions and shortcomings of this essay are the author's exclusive responsibility.

failure is, after all, in the eyes of the beholder. Co-ops are frequently evaluated according to externally imposed quantitative standards, like profit rates and technical efficiency. These evaluations often fail to capture qualitative benefits and nonmaterial goals that members may deem important as well, such as life satisfaction and influence in the community (Wells 1981). Also, the fact that many producers have previously abandoned their co-ops does not mean that they will never participate in others. As the cases analyzed in this chapter show, some producers are forming new co-ops and collective institutions for economic governance, drawing on their previous experiences in "bad" organizations to help them build "good" ones.

Although the criticisms of co-ops are warranted to an extent, the gloomy views of their role in the future of rural Mexico are not. Understanding why some co-ops succeed while others fail remains an important subject. This chapter examines two successful rural co-ops in Baja California, exploring how they formed as well as the conditions that helped them consolidate and improve their performance.[1] The discussion addresses the following questions. What factors initially motivated individual producers to cooperate with others? How did they look for and select each other? How did they decide about the size of their organizations and the scope of their cooperation? What enabled them to solve collective action problems? How has their cooperation evolved?

The analysis suggests that four factors helped individual producers cooperate and associate: (1) a perception of threats and opportunities to which producers could respond only if they worked with others; (2) preexisting bonds of trust among individuals that enabled them to meet with others to discuss and design collective projects; (3) the restriction of entry into the emerging group to ensure the fiduciary responsibility and technical competence of all members, and the restriction of group size to balance economies of scale and transaction costs; and (4) the development of an institutional framework that gave producers incentives to comply with their commitments to each other.

These facilitating conditions reduced risks, uncertainty, and transaction costs, and therefore enabled cooperative exchanges. They help

---

[1] This study is based on approximately forty open-ended interviews in 1995 and 1996 with members of the two co-ops, government officials, private consultants, and leaders of the Federation of Ejido Fishing Production Units (FUPPE) and the National Peasants' Confederation (CNC). The basic approach is comparative, focusing on the similarities and differences between the two cases. The research also benefited from internal documents of the co-ops as well as secondary data from the Trust Fund for Shared Risk (FIRCO) and the Ministry of the Environment, Natural Resources, and Fisheries (SEMARNAP).

account for the emergence and subsequent success of these co-ops. At the same time, the absence of these factors could explain why efforts to establish co-ops elsewhere in rural Mexico have been less successful.

Fishermen and Farmers: The Cases

The first of the two cases studies is the Mortera de Leyva Grupo "A." Established in 1986, this rural production society (SPR) consists of twenty-two sea urchin fishermen in the rural community of El Rosario, municipality of Ensenada. Mortera is one of the founding organizations of a federation of fishing co-ops in Baja California, the Federation of Ejido Fishing Production Units (FUPPE), affiliated to the National Peasants' Confederation (CNC) of Mexico's ruling Institutional Revolutionary Party (PRI).

The second case study is the Grupo Agroindustrial VIC-TOR. Established in 1993, this is a civil association (SC) comprising twenty-three wheat and cotton farmers, located in the rural community of Paredones, municipality of Mexicali. Over half of its members belong to the Victoria and Torreón ejidos, which explains the name of their co-op (VIC-TOR). In contrast to Mortera, VIC-TOR is not affiliated with a political party.

Mortera and VIC-TOR were selected because of the remarkable successes they have achieved. Both co-ops have fulfilled the initial objectives for which they were established: securing fishing permits and improving marketing in the case of the fishermen, and obtaining access to credit in the case of the farmers.[2] Furthermore, both co-ops have moved beyond these initial goals by launching new, highly profitable activities, such as processing and input procurement. As a result, the incomes of *all* members have increased substantially. This equitable distribution of benefits is unusual for these kinds of producer organizations, where benefits are often concentrated among the leaders and the better off.

In addition, both co-ops have increased their memberships' participation and influence in the broader community. For instance, Mortera's administrator was recently elected municipal councilor, and its members were leading local efforts to improve schools and public infrastructure in El Rosario. Likewise, VIC-TOR's president

---

[2] For a description of general conditions and problems in the sea urchin industry in Baja California, see Arredondo Gómez 1994. For the farming sector, see Magaña Magaña 1994.

was on the board of the state government's development planning agency and the Farmers Council.

Finally, Mortera and VIC-TOR are especially intriguing cases because their members were previously affiliated with large, powerful co-ops. The producers who founded Mortera and VIC-TOR withdrew from these earlier co-ops because they considered them manipulative and exploitative, benefiting a small elite group rather than the rank and file. Remarkably, despite their strong negative opinion about their former co-ops, the members of Mortera and VIC-TOR chose to embark on new collective ventures. The evidence indicates that these producers learned from their prior experience with "bad" co-ops what *not* to do in their new ones.[3] Hence the cases of Mortera and VIC-TOR offer important insights into how producers' previous experiences with failed or partially successful co-ops may help, rather than hinder, their subsequent cooperative efforts.

The Fishermen of Mortera

Initial Objectives: Fishing Permits and Collective Marketing

Like other species of the rich littoral of Baja California, such as lobster, abalone, and sea cucumber, the red sea urchin commands a very high price. The Baja peninsula is the only place in Mexico with a red sea urchin fishery, and all the production is exported to Japan via the United States.[4] Commercial exploitation of the sea urchin began in the early 1970s, when Japanese fishermen and traders came to Baja California to teach fishing techniques to the locals and to open channels for commercialization. Today the sector comprises about 800 fishermen and creates approximately another 1,200 jobs distributed among rural production societies, ejidal fishing production units (UPPEs), cooperatives, and private firms. Total exports from the peninsula

---

[3] Moreover, in recent years other producers in the region have followed the example of these two pioneer co-ops, forming quite successful organizations, which suggests there is nothing unique to Mortera and VIC-TOR and that some of their basic features may be replicable.

[4] The red sea urchin (*Strongylocentrotus franciscanus*) is an animal with a globular body covered by spines whose gonads are suitable for human consumption. Japan is virtually the only consumer, with a demand estimated between three and five tons per day. The main producers are Japan, Mexico, Chile, the United States, Canada, Norway, Ireland, France, Denmark, Russia, China, South Korea, and the Philippines. In the case of Mexico, the production is exported to Japan via the United States mainly due to issues of sanitary certification and handling. See Arredondo Gómez 1994; Payeiro Nayar 1982.

generate between U.S.$4 and 6 million annually (SEMARNAP 1995; Arredondo Gómez 1994).

During the 1970s and 1980s, producers affiliated with a handful of cooperatives did most of the fishing of high-priced species. Among these organizations, the largest and most influential was Cooperativa Ensenada, which controlled the marketing of abalone, lobster, sea urchin, and other species captured in El Rosario and neighboring communities.[5] Cooperativa Ensenada was supposed to benefit all of its members, but many felt that most gains went to the caciques and a small elite, ultimately impoverishing the rank and file. Discontented members criticized Cooperativa Ensenada for a broad range of problems, including bad management, shady deals, arbitrary prices for products, insufficient retirement funds, and political manipulation. According to one of Mortera's founders:

> The caciques controlled everything. Our product had no value for us, even though we knew that the lobster, the abalone, and the sea urchin had good prices abroad. But that money never filtered down to us, always living in paperboard houses and badly clothed.... And if you retired, they gave you a kick in the rear. My father retired after thirty years of work and received just 3,000 pesos.[6]

This situation worsened in the early 1980s, when years of overfishing of sea urchin resulted in reduced production and the exhaustion of several fishing banks, threatening the survival of the species and the subsistence of many fishermen.[7] A profound sense of crisis developed among the fishermen.

During 1983 and 1984, several families of fishermen in El Rosario and Ejido Uruapan started to meet and search for alternatives. They saw no use in fighting against the caciques for control of the cooperative, because the power relationship was very asymmetric. They also discarded the idea of forming a new cooperative, because the local caciques would easily have blocked their efforts, and the na-

---

[5] Founded in 1938 during the government of President Lázaro Cárdenas, Cooperativa Ensenada represented a cornerstone of the system of fishing co-ops in Mexico. It incorporated virtually every fishing community along 400 miles of the peninsular littoral, including El Rosario. All the fishermen that created Mortera were previously affiliated with Cooperativa Ensenada.

[6] In the early 1980s, 3,000 pesos were worth between 50 and 100 U.S. dollars.

[7] Overfishing was related to the low prices fishermen were receiving for their product, so that they tended to compensate by capturing large volumes. By the mid-1980s, several co-ops had begun to lobby the government to limit the annual fishing season to nine months—July to March—and to monitor the sea urchin population in the littoral. See SEMARNAP 1995.

tional leadership of the CNC would not have supported such an initiative.

Then a window of opportunity opened for these disgruntled fishermen. They discovered that the federal agrarian law allowed for semi-independent "ejido production units" to be formed if they were supported by the ejido authorities—and it happened that some of the fishermen who were critical of Cooperativa Ensenada held positions in the commissariat of one of the two ejidos in El Rosario. Also, unlike the lobster and the abalone, the sea urchin was not among the species reserved by law for cooperatives, and hence it could be harvested by private producers or, alternatively, by ejido production units.[8]

However, the fishermen who sought to break free of Cooperativa Ensenada faced an important challenge: the local market for sea urchin was firmly under the control of the Cooperativa, a few private producers, and a few traders from Ensenada. Had these fishermen tried to work individually, it would have been easy for their political adversaries and economic competitors to boycott their sales. Moreover, officials from the federal Ministry of the Environment, Natural Resources, and Fisheries (SEMARNAP) told them they would need the support of the governor of Baja California to get fishing permits, support they could only secure if they were united and organized.[9]

In short, the circumstances under which the fishermen of El Rosario and Ejido Uruapan sought to exit Cooperative Ensenada forced them to establish a significant degree of market power and political strength—tasks they could not achieve individually. Cooperation was imperative if they wanted to survive as producers.

Trust: The Importance of Family Ties

Most members of Cooperativa Ensenada faced similar problems. Why did the fishermen of Mortera form a new, autonomous organization while others did not? This author argues that trust—that is, the

---

[8] The agrarian law at the time was not specific about the organization of ejido production units for fishing, but it certainly did not preclude such units from forming. Mortera and other allied groups later lobbied the national Congress to fill the vacuums and create the legal entity UPPE.

[9] If Ministry inspectors caught somebody fishing or selling sea urchin without a permit, that person would be legally liable and could lose all fishing permits. The state governor, Xicoténcatl Leyva Mortera, eventually supported these fishermen, helping them get the permits and giving them U.S.$2,000 to $3,000 to rent additional equipment. As a sign of appreciation and to show others they had his support, the fishermen named the co-op after the governor's mother.

willingness to expose oneself to the consequences of someone else's actions—was a key factor that helped this group of fishermen get together and start discussing collective projects.

The strongest, almost unconditional trust usually develops in families and small communities (see Luhmann 1988; Barber 1983). When societies grow and become more complex, the preservation of this natural reliance among individuals through kinship, ethnic background, religion, and so on, forms a basis for *ascribed trust* (Schmitz 1996). In industrial clusters, trading networks, and co-ops all over the world, ascribed trust generated by sociocultural ties serves to minimize the risk of opportunistic behavior, reduce transaction costs, and improve economic performance.

Ascribed trust based on family ties eased the way for individual producers in El Rosario and Ejido Uruapan to get together and cooperate. Mortera is virtually a family business—the business of the Espinozas. The fishermen who founded Mortera first met to analyze their situation and discuss fighting against the caciques and leaving Cooperativa Ensenada—sensitive matters indeed—inside the Espinoza family circle, where they had the most solidarity and mutual reliance. Today, fifteen of the twenty-two producers affiliated with Mortera are brothers or cousins within the extended Espinoza family; the rest are close friends, having grown up together with the Espinozas, who regard them "as if they were family."[10] According to one of Mortera's members:

> All of us are family in these groups because there's just a few people. You don't have problems of lawsuits or that sort of thing; nor do you have the heart to say, "I'm going to screw them all." Because how am I going to screw my brothers, my cousins, or my friends, or how are they going to screw me?

Restricting Entry and Size: Membership Selection and Coordination

After they decided to leave Cooperativa Ensenada, the promoters of the new co-op arranged formal meetings to discuss their ideas and projects with a broader group of producers. Promoters say the invi-

---

[10] The Espinozas have lived in El Rosario since the early 1800s and are the most important clan in the region. In the course of the years, other families have arrived and intermarried with the Espinozas. These families have buried their dead together, fought the same fights to defend their land, and, not surprisingly, worked on the same fisheries. Even for a small town like this, it is difficult to imagine a deeper sense of belonging. See Espinoza Arroyo 1992.

tations were open to "everybody"—meaning all the discontented fishermen in El Rosario affiliated with Cooperativa Ensenada—so that nobody could say they wanted to exclude people or to do things in secret. This reduced the universe of potential participants to a relatively small number of well-known people, probably between 100 and 120. However, it seems that personal invitations were restricted to "trustworthy, like-minded, hard-working people," and probably about 50 to 60 producers participated in the initial meetings. In the end, 40 producers actually joined the new co-op, and most were either members of the Espinoza family or close friends.

Why would fishermen want to restrict entry to their co-op? Would a more inclusive and larger membership not have generated greater political clout and lowered production costs? Part of the question relates again to the notion of trust, but with a different take. Trustworthiness can be understood in terms of *fiduciary responsibility*—that is, the expectation that all parties to an exchange are *willing* to live up to their commitments—as well as in terms of *technical competence*—that is, the expectation that people are *able* to live up to these commitments.[11] People who want to cooperate and associate with others can establish selection criteria to help ensure that everyone involved would be willing and able to comply with their collective contracts. These criteria may vary according to the needs and risks of their projects.

Terms such as "trustworthy, like-minded, hard-working people" may seem too vague to serve as reliable selection criteria, but in a community like El Rosario—where virtually everyone knows everything about the rest—they are not. Besides, the fishermen's initial cooperative tasks did not require producers to meet high standards of technical competence: they needed to join forces to get the governor's support and fishing permits from SEMARNAP, goals that had more to do with fiduciary responsibility and solidarity than with competence. Once they got permits, the producers would fish in independent teams and loosely coordinate to market their products.

Restricting entry makes sense from the perspective of fiduciary responsibility and technical competence. Still, why would fishermen want to restrict the size of their group if that meant forgoing benefi-

---

[11] See Barber 1983. Expectations of fiduciary responsibility are highly subjective. They are usually based on knowledge and interpretation of past experience, or on the notion that it is better to rely on "certain kinds" of people than on others. On the other hand, expectations for technical competence can be more objective. They are based on the minimal standards and characteristics that producers must fulfill in order to make collective projects viable. These requirements might relate to financial capacity and soundness, technological endowments, market access, knowledge, and so on, depending on the nature of each particular project.

cial economies of scale as well? In cooperative scenarios, economies of scale occur when individuals pool their assets and/or productive capabilities, lowering average costs and raising returns for the group and for themselves. However, just as corporations experience diseconomies in terms of management and flexibility as they get very large, co-ops may also experience diseconomies as a consequence of aggregating more members: they become increasingly complex and difficult to coordinate as their membership expands. Furthermore, the transaction costs arising from taking decisions, combining resources, distributing gains, and keeping people accountable are likely to increase with membership size as well. Thus, economic gains depend on striking a balance between economies and diseconomies of scale.[12]

With respect to diseconomies of scale and maximum size, during the preparatory meetings the promoters of Mortera realized that as more people participated, it would be harder to organize and take decisions together. They reasoned that a large group would be difficult to coordinate, and so they stopped inviting people when they felt the group was getting too big. Finally, twenty-nine people associated in 1986, some of them providing moral and political support but never actually making economic contributions to the group. In the following years additional people joined and others left the co-op, and by 1996 the co-op numbered twenty-two members.[13]

Institutions for Internal Governance: Self-Enforcing Agreements, Flexible Sanctions, and Rules

Before moving forward it is convenient to clarify some of the arguments outlined above. This author argues that trust was an important factor for fishermen to get together, organize, and start developing collective projects. That is not to say that trust alone was enough for them to initiate and sustain cooperation; it was also necessary for them to believe that it was in everyone's *self-interest* to fulfill their

---

[12] Wade (1988) suggests that in collective organizations, the likelihood of success depends on the size of the group: the smaller the number of members, the better the chances of success, down to a minimum below which the tasks able to be performed by such a small group cease to be meaningful. Olson (1977) also argues that the smaller the group, the more its members will have incentives to see that it does not fail. He also suggests that social pressure to hold people accountable functions better when groups are small.

[13] Most of the other fifteen to twenty co-ops that later split from Cooperativa Ensenada also have between fifteen and thirty-four members, a fact that possibly hints at the size co-ops must have to work efficiently in this context.

cooperative commitments. Institutions have an important bearing on the definition of self-interest. They set "the rules of the game" in a society, and they establish an incentive scheme that provides stability and meaning to social behavior (North 1990). Institutions include formal restrictions such as laws, informal restrictions such as norms and social conventions, and enforcement mechanisms such as monitoring systems and sanctions. Institutions matter for economic performance because they reduce uncertainty in exchange relations, thus shaping the transaction costs and the efficiency of collective action.[14]

Institutions have played a fundamental role in Mortera's success. The fishermen developed an incentive structure that placed substantial benefits on compliance with cooperative agreements and substantial costs on breaching them. Perhaps Mortera's most important institution is a self-enforcing agreement about collective marketing.[15] When the fishermen were about to formalize the co-op, they understood that the benefits from cooperation would be very substantial,[16] yet they realized they could only achieve these benefits if they captured and jointly sold sufficiently large amounts of sea urchin. Therefore, they agreed to exclude members if they failed to produce for more than two months or if they sold their product outside the co-op.

From the perspective of an opportunistic individual, fishing with the co-op's assets but selling the catch on his own might seem very profitable, because that individual would reap the full value of the product while sharing the costs with the rest of the group. However, it would not be easy for such a "free rider" to sell outside the co-op without the knowledge of the other members. First, fishing is carried out in teams, so the prospective free rider would have to bribe at least

---

[14] In this view, transaction costs are the "frictions" between exchanging parties, whereas institutions and trust are "lubricants." See Williamson 1985.

[15] An agreement is self-enforcing if the threat to terminate transactions and the subsequent loss of business if one party is caught cheating are sufficient to deter opportunism and ensure that contractual obligations are met. These types of agreements arise in many situations where it is difficult and costly to depend on third parties, such as the judiciary system, to enforce contracts and assess losses when they are not honored. See Telser 1980.

[16] First of all, producers would get the fishing permits necessary to produce. Those that had equipment would team up with others that did not have any (these teammates would be paid as associates and not as employees, favoring a more egalitarian distribution of gains), and they would rent additional equipment and share existing equipment if necessary. They also planned to process the sea urchin in the near future, adding considerable value to it. Most important, producers would get better prices and higher profits than in Cooperativa Ensenada. Besides, the Leóns in Ejido Uruapan and the Vieras in El Rosario had recently started fishing other species outside Cooperativa Ensenada, and the fact that they were having good results encouraged the Espinozas to form their own co-op as well.

two more people, thereby risking secrecy and cutting profits. Second, there are virtually no buying outlets nearby that would assure a potential free rider confidentiality, so that individual would probably have to take the product to Ensenada, which is more than 200 miles away. Finally, because of its small size and close-knit associational structure, El Rosario closely approximates a world of perfect information. In such a context, it might be easier to hide and freeze a passing gray whale than several barrels of sea urchin! Thus the chances of getting away with cheating would be slim. Furthermore, the cheater would lack the infrastructure for processing the sea urchin and would have to sell it live, losing much of its potential value.

Consequently, net gains from cheating probably would not exceed by much what the individual would receive from the co-op, considering that its products sell in better markets at higher prices. On the contrary, a cheater's potential losses would be very high, primarily because of the economic benefits lost by expulsion but also in social terms—that is, alienation from family and friends. The evidence suggests that Mortera's self-enforcing agreement works: no cheating has been detected since the early 1990s.

The fishermen of El Rosario have also worked to establish effective sanctions against opportunistic behavior that could undermine their co-op's viability and performance. For example, Mortera forbids its members from fishing unauthorized species or fishing in other people's banks because, if government regulators discover such behavior, the co-op as a whole could lose its permits. Individuals who violate these rules are punished by expulsion. Other kinds of behavior merit less severe sanctions. For example, the leader of a fishing team once ruined the motor of a co-op boat. Team leaders pay for their own engine oil, and this leader tried to save money by using cheap automotive oil instead of the more expensive oil for outboard motors. The motor failed and was taken to a mechanic, who told Mortera's administrator what had caused the problem. The co-op's administrative council could have expelled this individual for his negligence and greed, but it chose instead to have him pay for the motor in twelve monthly installments withheld from his earnings.

Just as Mortera has sanctions to prevent opportunism, it also has rules to ensure that members reap the benefits of cooperating. Cooperativa Ensenada paid producers 50 percent of the expected selling price of their product in advance. At the end of the year, after covering production costs, remaining revenues were distributed as profits. But the administrators of Cooperativa Ensenada often set expected prices arbitrarily and reported a selling price lower than the actual one, thus cheating producers. In contrast, Mortera pays a fixed price in advance that leaves producers with good money in their pockets.

The administrative council participates in the negotiations with buyers and has to report the final selling price to the membership. Furthermore, the oversight council regularly reviews the terms of selling contracts.[17] The remaining revenues are distributed as profits at the end of the year, after covering operating costs and contributions to the retirement fund. These arrangements make the distribution of benefits more transparent and legitimate.

Problems and Consolidation

The four factors analyzed above helped the fishermen cooperate and rapidly accomplish their initial goals. In light of their early success, cooperation expanded to other profitable activities. Aside from fishing and marketing, today Mortera also has its own retirement fund and factories to process sea urchin.[18] Moreover, in the late 1980s and early 1990s it joined forces with other fishing co-ops to move up the commodity chain. They first bypassed the intermediaries from Ensenada, and they later allied with a Japanese trader to establish an exporting company in San Diego, bypassing U.S. intermediaries and selling directly to Japan.

Despite these successes, Mortera has had serious internal problems and conflicts. In the early years most things went well. The fishing was good, the co-op was processing sea urchin and selling it to the U.S. intermediaries, and members' earnings were on the rise. But the 1990 season was quite poor due to adverse ecological conditions in the fishing banks. Mortera could barely pay for basic expenses, generating frictions among members and making some of them distrust the co-op's administration. The situation turned into conflict, and more than a dozen members decided to leave and form a new co-op—Grupo Reforma Agraria Integral.[19] They were replaced by the sons and brothers of the remaining members, and the situation

---

[17] The administrator, the administrative council, and the oversight council are democratically elected by the assembly of members, which holds them accountable and can sanction or dismiss them at any time if they become negligent or dishonest.

[18] During the fishing season, Mortera usually employs twelve to twenty workers to process the product, paying them between U.S.$6 and $8 per hour. At the peak of the season—from July to mid–October—employees can easily earn U.S.$700 a month, and some even earn more than $1,000.

[19] The members who left Mortera in 1990 were tied to two nuclear families within the Espinoza clan—the Acevedos and the Peraltas—while most of those who stayed were from a third family—the Arroyos, the original promoters of the co-op. This suggests that there is a connection between patterns of exit/loyalty and family ties at the nuclear level.

of the co-op improved again when the fishing banks recovered. One member assessed the problem as follows:

> When people feel weak and have problems, they look to others for support. But once they've got money and feel strong, they start complaining and [think they can do everything by themselves]. They think it's easier just to break away.... That's what happened to us, and the same has happened to other co-ops.... It's this lack of culture and solidarity that sometimes just doesn't let us progress.

The four factors examined in preceding sections did not impede this split, but they have helped the fishermen deal with other problems. For instance, family ties and trust have helped them manage minor disagreements. The members have also established specific conflict management mechanisms, as one of them describes:

> We agreed and set as a rule that there wouldn't be any verbal attacks or denunciations against other members without cause: "when you make an accusation, you have to explain the cause and present proof of it to the assembly." We did this because there were many attacks, especially from those who left, who almost always were the laziest.

In recent years, Mortera has not had any problem grave enough to undermine cooperation among its members, perhaps because the fishing seasons have been good and the gains substantial and well distributed: in 1995–1996 members earned an average of U.S.$10,000 to $12,000, and a producer received $10,000 from Mortera's retirement fund, in addition to his corresponding annual profits.

Other co-ops have recently emerged in El Rosario and neighboring communities, most of them also organized around families. Three families in particular—the Espinozas and the Vieras from El Rosario, and the Leóns from Ejido Uruapan—have become powerful economic and political allies. They opened the way for other people to leave Cooperativa Ensenada, established the marketing channel to Japan, and organized the FUPPE—a federation of twenty-two ejido fishing production units, rural production societies, and cooperatives. Backed by the federation and allied with other peasant groups, they challenged and almost overthrew the traditional leadership of the CNC at the municipal and state levels.[20]

---

[20] The sociocultural ties between these three clans are not as strong as those binding the members in each of them, and their ties with the rest of the federated co-ops are weaker still. This suggests that the federation is actually a network of strong *and* weak

The Farmers of VIC-TOR

Initial Objective: Access to Credit

In the early 1990s, the situation in the Mexicali Valley was characterized by intriguing contradictions. Agricultural production was on the
rise, due in part to exports of vegetables like asparagus and green
onions. However, there was a whitefly plague, and the prices for
wheat and cotton, by far the most important crops in the valley, were
still low relative to the costs of production and the opportunity cost
of labor.[21] Many small farmers—normally holding around twenty
hectares—were not able to pay or restructure their overdue accounts
with BANRURAL, the federal government's agricultural development
bank. Renting privately owned and ejido land became widespread,
with unofficial estimates at about 70 or 80 percent of the total parcels.[22]

By 1992, the farmers who would found VIC-TOR the following
year had already left the traditional cooperative system. The majority
had been affiliated previously with Cooperativa Luis Echeverría Ál-
varez (LEA), one of the richest and most powerful co-ops in north-
western Mexico during the 1970s and early 1980s but very much
weakened by the 1990s.[23] They left LEA because they considered it
inefficient and its leaders corrupt. Furthermore, they had repaid their
prior BANRURAL loans and were thus eligible for fresh credits—in
contrast to many LEA members who were in default and needed the
organization to lobby for them. Also, most of the farmers who chose
to withdraw from LEA produced wheat, a staple controlled by
CONASUPO—the government's staple food procurement agency—so
they had outlets besides LEA through which to sell their harvest. Fi-

---

ties, a combination likely to enhance its overall economic and political power. See
Granovetter 1973 for an elaboration on strong and weak ties.

[21] Mexicali is next to the Imperial and Cochella valleys and just four hours from Los
Angeles, places that employ large quantities of immigrant labor, both legal and illegal. Family and friends across the border often serve as a network for employment,
and therefore many people in the Mexicali Valley have the option to work in the
United States for much higher wages than at home.

[22] Getting an accurate estimate for rented land is problematic because most contracts are
informal or unrecorded. However, the estimates above are widely accepted among
government officials, researchers, and private consultants.

[23] LEA was established in the early 1970s and was affiliated with the CNC. Its leadership allied with other CNC–affiliated co-op and ejido leaders throughout the state of
Baja California—including Cooperativa Ensenada. Until recently, LEA leaders had
political control of the majority of rural communities in Baja California. LEA was
weakened in the late 1980s and early 1990s due to widespread corruption and inefficiency, as well as important changes in the valley's economy.

nally, these farmers had survived the economic problems afflicting the Mexicali Valley without having to rent out their own land or resort to renting other people's land. For these reasons, they thought they would be able to achieve greater success on their own than as members of LEA.

However, the outlook for these ex–LEA affiliates started to change for the worse in late 1992. First, the Mexican Congress was reforming Article 27 of the Constitution, which created much uncertainty about the future of ejidatarios and rural debtors in general. Second, some of the farmers had difficulties renewing their production loans, even though they had repaid their debts. Furthermore, they learned that other small farmers were encountering similar problems. Based on this experience, the farmers reasoned that credit policies were tightening and might get worse. They worried about the prospects for getting credit the following year and felt themselves at risk, because without credit they would be unable to produce.

These farmers also perceived that the tightening of rural credit by government and private banks was not affecting all producers the same way. They saw that owners and renters with larger landholdings—100 hectares and up—were more likely to get loans than small farmers.[24] So if they could somehow become "larger," they would be in a much better position to secure credit. The problem was how to achieve such an increase in scale, given that they lacked the money to buy or rent more land and were unwilling to give up the rights to their land to form a commune. They came up with a plausible alternative: associate with other creditworthy farmers and submit a single, comprehensive credit application, with enough people for BANRURAL officials to feel sufficiently confident—and pressured—to approve the loan. The association would give credit to the associates, who would pay it back so that the association could repay the bank.

As one of the initial promoters of VIC-TOR put it:

> Although we have a system to manage our own affairs individually ... our idea was to get together to do what none of us could do alone—in this case, to secure credit. That's it ... and that's been our motto ever since.

---

[24] Their reasoning went as follows. First, large producers would have lower costs and more profits than small ones, thereby reducing default risk. Second, banks would prefer to lend to larger producers because it would be easier and cheaper to issue and monitor a single deal of 100 hectares than 5 deals of 20. Finally, larger credit deals open more opportunities for bank officials to enrich themselves. According to VIC-TOR farmers, word of mouth and the experience of several large producers confirmed their intuition.

In the case of VIC-TOR, cooperation emerged from shared self-interest. As we shall see, there was little sense of solidarity or altruism among the farmers: if they could have secured credit on their own, they would not have formed an association.

Trust: Family Ties and Individual Reputations

The advantages of cooperation were very clear to the farmers, but so were the risks and problems it implied. After all, if somebody failed to repay their portion of the group credit, the rest would have to make up the difference. Therefore, it was natural for them to be skeptical about associating. Trust reduced this initial skepticism and enabled farmers to get together, share ideas, and start developing their project.

Trust among the farmers was ascribed as well as earned. Ascribed trust was rooted in social relations. *Earned* trust, by contrast, stemmed mainly from economic activities (Schmitz 1996). Ascribed trust had a familial basis: at the time of VIC-TOR's initial meetings in early 1993, about half of the members were relatives, *compadres* (fictive kin), or close friends. Family ties were not concentrated in a single clan but were dispersed among various small groups not directly connected with each other.

Earned trust was based on the reputation for honesty, competence, and hard work that some farmers had established in their own communities. Just a few farmers had a positive reputation that everybody else acknowledged; some were acknowledged as good producers by only a few other participants. That was because, though all lived in the Paredones region, the farmers were scattered across six different communities and ejidos and not all of them knew one another.

How could the participants in VIC-TOR's first meetings have trusted each other at all if most did not really know each other? These individuals were embedded in a social network, with connections based on familiarity and reputation. The three or four initial promoters of VIC-TOR formed the core trunk of the network; from each of them extend various branches, and from some of these, more branches. Consequently, although not all the participants were connected to each other directly, everybody was connected at least indirectly. These connections provided a basis for a minimum level of trust among the farmers, because each could say, "I don't trust you, but I trust somebody who does."

This low level of trust makes the case of VIC-TOR especially intriguing from a policy perspective: if these farmers were able to associate successfully despite their initial skepticism, it might be that they *did* something to build trust. That is precisely the topic explored in the following sections.

Restricting Entry and Size

In addition to helping identify and recruit potential members, the social network that undergirded VIC-TOR also served to restrict entry to the new organization. Invitations to join VIC-TOR were extended via preexisting social ties; a promoter invited his comadre, she brought a well-respected farmer from her community, and so on.

The criteria for membership in VIC-TOR explicitly combined elements of fiduciary responsibility and technical competence. Not just any comadre or relative was invited to join, only those considered to be successful, honest producers. This might explain why VIC-TOR's membership included no more than three or four members of a single family. Furthermore, considering that they would apply for a consolidated loan, they required everyone to have credit and the capacity to repay it. One of VIC-TOR's original promoters recounts:

> We looked for people [with affinity], that spoke the same language and liked to work. It was select people ... who didn't have credit problems and had been characterized, despite the problems we had, as being productive.... You can't start a group [like ours] with a member who has credit problems.

There was an additional selection mechanism that shaped the composition of VIC-TOR's membership. Everyone had to put money down for the initial capital and registration fees of the co-op, as well as for the honorariums of the consulting firm—Alianza Consultoria Integral—that was helping them formalize and register the co-op.[25] Thus only individuals who were willing to make a significant financial commitment to the organization could join.

As for the restriction on size, farmers got an idea of the number of members the co-op should have through the experiences of larger producers on both sides of the U.S.–Mexico border, as well as from their own prior participation in ejido assemblies. According to one of VIC-TOR's founding leaders:

> We needed 500 hectares. Why? Because in 500 hectares you can land any project; with less, you can't. You can buy inputs cheaper, you can buy a tractor and pay it easily, you can buy a threshing machine and pay it back just like that,

---

[25] The role of the consultants is discussed in a later section.

> because of the payment capacity you have when you come
> together [with others]. Why not more than 500 [hectares]?
> Because if we go for more than 500, we go above 25 mem-
> bers, which is the ideal for us.... As long as every person
> has a different mentality, if you put 50 or more people in a
> meeting it becomes a melee and it's difficult to concert and
> work things out. We thought that 22 to 25 was a manage-
> able, not very problematic number.

This statement suggests that farmers had a clear notion of economies
of scale in agricultural production and an intuition about how transaction costs shaped the prospects for collective action. They figured
out how to balance the incentives to grow (maximizing economies of
scale) with the incentives to remain small (minimizing transaction
costs), thereby increasing their chances of success.

Institutions for Monitoring and Sanctioning

Once the membership and size of the group were established, the
farmers shifted their attention to defining an institutional framework
that would give order and stability to their collective activities. It was
especially important for them to establish effective deterrents against
opportunistic behavior, because of the high risks of the project and
the members' low levels of initial trust. Therefore, they designed a
framework for governance that—in contrast to Mortera's—relied
mainly on formal rules, sanctions, and third-party enforcement,
rather than on informal norms and self-enforcing agreements.

In designing VIC-TOR's institutions, the farmers drew on their
previous experiences in LEA and the ejido governing bodies. According to one participant:

> Here everything takes into account the *mañas* [bad habits or
> vices] we found in other places.... For example, there are
> still people out there thinking that [the leaders] are going
> to end up millionaires [as in LEA]. But here there are 8
> people that propose and 23 that decide. In the group, the
> president or the administrative council cannot get a credit
> just like that; they must have the authorization of all the as-
> sociates before taking a single peso from the bank.

Farmers wanted to prevent opportunism among leaders and managers as well as among the membership. Above all, they wanted to
make sure that nobody would fail to repay his installment of the collective loan, because VIC-TOR would be liable for the defaulted
amount. Therefore, farmers established punitive and pecuniary sanc-

tions to prevent this kind of cheating. If somebody did not pay and had no good reason for failing to do so, the co-op would expel him and retain enough of his corresponding capital and profits to make up for the debt. If his share of capital and profits did not suffice, VIC-TOR would take control of his land and use it until the debt was fully paid. However, if he had a valid reason for his inability to pay, the rest of the members would discuss his case and take appropriate action. This is what one farmer said about credit repayment and sanctions:

> Just to illustrate how serious and maybe even rigid we are about these things, if somebody makes bad use of the credit, he's automatically out, but his land still serves as collateral for the money he made bad use of.... But if he loses the harvest and it is not his fault—say, a plague or something—we have the money to say, "you don't owe anything," and we pay for him.

For example, one farmer almost lost his harvest and, had VIC-TOR not intervened, likely would have defaulted. He had planted the seeds too deep, and they failed to germinate. The members decided to help him: in just three days a group of them brought their tractors, replowed the land, and planted new seed. This time the farmer got sprouts and a harvest, and VIC-TOR members spared themselves a problem.

VIC-TOR's institutional framework is dynamic: at least every six months the membership holds an assembly to review the internal rules of operation, so that these can be adapted to new needs and opportunities. They have come up with a framework that combines monitoring mechanisms to prevent corruption and sanctions to punish cheating, while at the same time allowing for flexibility and solidarity in case of misfortune. On the whole, this institutional framework has given members appropriate incentives to comply with their collective commitments, helping them sustain cooperation.

Problems and Consolidation

Despite their notable successes sustaining cooperation, VIC-TOR's farmers have repeatedly faced problems of uncooperative attitudes and behavior. Two of the twenty-five original members have left the co-op. One was the former treasurer, who left because—according to some members—"he just did not get the idea of the group" and wanted to profit from his position. The other was a better-off farmer who "was accustomed to managing his business his own way and did not really need the group." The first case generated some trouble for the co-op; the second did not. These cases suggest that cooperation is difficult to sustain when people do not want to live by the rules or when the rules do not live up to what people expect.

Obviously, some VIC-TOR members are more skeptical and individualistic than others, and therefore less motivated to cooperate. What is interesting is that these producers increasingly seem to have *learned* to cooperate based on the experience of others. For instance, while in the first season everybody sold the harvest on their own, by the second season seven producers sold together, reaching better markets and getting better prices than the rest. In light of their success, by the third season everybody sold their harvests together. Something similar happened with the procurement of inputs: at first nobody bought them together, later fifteen did and saved money, and finally everybody did.

Although gaining access to credit for working capital was the original reason for the farmers to associate, success in that area opened new opportunities. During the first season, they only joined forces to get the collective loan, but two years later they were also working together to sell their wheat at higher prices, buy inputs and services more cheaply, and produce their own seed. They had gotten grants and long-term loans from the state government, BANRURAL, and the Trust Fund for Shared Risk (FIRCO) to buy a tractor with laser-guided leveling equipment, to acquire vacuum tanks for fertilizer, and to build storage facilities. They had even started their own insurance fund. Farmers calculated that by the organization's third year, profits for individual producers were about 50 percent higher than they would have been had the farmers not formed VIC-TOR, and the initial value of the co-op's shares had grown at least sevenfold in real terms. Moreover, for the 1996 season they expected to market wheat from other co-ops and individual campesinos. In short, cooperation has clearly been good business.

VIC-TOR's relations with external actors merit some comment. After several preparatory meetings, the farmers contacted a consulting firm—Alianza Consultoria Integral—to assist them with the legal dimensions of their collective credit application. But soon the main consultant—an agronomist and former BANRURAL official—was helping them structure the co-op's productive operations and internal rules as well, so that together they identified new windows of opportunity for the farmers. Alianza assisted VIC-TOR in feasibility studies and negotiation of grants and loans with government agencies and BANRURAL. After its experience and success with VIC-TOR, Alianza started helping other similar groups in the Mexicali Valley. The story of VIC-TOR and Alianza suggests that external agents with expertise and capacity for political mediation can effectively support the start-up and development of co-ops.[26]

Conclusion

Four factors facilitated cooperation in these two successful co-ops. The first has to do with threats, opportunities and shared self-interest. The fishermen who came together to form Mortera felt exploited by the leaders of the large-scale, traditional co-op—Cooperativa Ensenada—with which they were affiliated. They realized that they could sell their sea urchin in more profitable markets by leaving Cooperativa Ensenada, but only if they joined together to obtain fishing permits and establish sufficient market power to avoid being boycotted by the old co-op and other competitors. The farmers who founded VIC-TOR felt threatened by the tightening of BAN-RURAL's credit and considered it vital to secure their future access to credit. To achieve this objective, they came together to make a joint loan application. In both cases, cooperation grew out of shared economic self-interest.

The second factor that helps account for the success of the two co-ops relates to trust. Producers recognized that cooperation entailed substantial risks and uncertainty, and therefore they were reluctant to cooperate. As the cases suggest, preexisting trust made it possible for producers to get together and formulate collective projects. The fishermen drew on ascribed trust rooted in strong family and community ties. The farmers, on the other hand, relied on trust anchored in a combination of family ties and individual reputations—that is, on both ascribed and earned trust.

The third factor concerns restrictions on group membership and size. Producers restricted entry to their new organizations based on evidence of fiduciary responsibility (*willingness* to comply with joint obligations) and technical competence (*capacity* to comply with joint obligations). Organizational size was limited intuitively, based on past experience and common sense about economies of scale and transaction costs: producers sought to balance economic incentives to expand their co-ops with organizational incentives to keep their co-ops small. These restrictions on entry and size, in turn, helped boost

---

[26] Wells (1982) suggests that broker agencies have played a similar role with producer co-ops in California. She argues that brokers can provide the information, communication skills, status, and sources of recommendation that are crucial to link co-ops with the larger economic and political system. Alianza provided such resources to VIC-TOR. Indeed, some government officials and bankers questioned whether VIC-TOR could have succeeded without Alianza's assistance.

members' confidence that their co-ops had the right people and the right scale to succeed.

The fourth factor involves institutions. To overcome obstacles to initiating and sustaining cooperation, producers needed not just to trust each other but also to believe that it was in their best interest to comply with collective commitments. Consequently, they built an institutional framework that constrained individual behavior and imposed order on their collective projects. They identified activities likely to foster opportunism—such as selling their product outside the organization in the case of the fishermen, and failing to repay credit in the case of the farmers—and crafted rules, agreements, and sanctions that gave members powerful incentives to forgo such activities. They also developed monitoring mechanisms to prevent corruption, and they enacted rules to ensure that everybody would benefit fairly from cooperation.

In addition to helping explain the emergence and success of Mortera and VIC-TOR, the four factors analyzed above could also help us understand why co-ops elsewhere either do not form or do not achieve their objectives. From a policy perspective, these four factors may serve as building blocks for an analytical approach to study and promote cooperation. Such an approach might be useful, for instance, to encourage cooperation among producers who have shared interests and bonds of trust. It could also serve to improve and consolidate existing co-ops by helping to identify crucial problems—inadequate rules, for example—and providing a framework for thinking about the solutions. Moreover, the approach might help diagnose and compare different groups and co-ops, thus helping target external assistance and resources in ways that maximize their impact.

Previous work suggests that sustained cooperation is often associated with a prior bond of trust among actors due to social milieu or reputation. Although the present findings support this view, the case of VIC-TOR suggests that prior levels of trust need not be high for people to cooperate and associate. That case suggests that groups with low levels of trust can compensate for this deficiency by deliberately making other conditions more stringent, such as those related to entry, size, and institutions. This compensation could reduce risk, uncertainty, and transaction costs, thereby making it easier to sustain cooperation.

It is very difficult to create trust, and hopefully nobody would try to worsen a situation just to induce collaboration—although worsening things has often been very easy. Fortunately, other conditions conducive to successful cooperation are also amenable to human manipulation. For instance, government agencies, nongovernmental organizations, and banks can generate and expand the rewards of cooperation by providing fiscal incentives, improving the supply of credit, or implementing preferential procurement programs for co-ops. Rural development agencies and universities can provide information and training for agricultural extensionists and private consultants, helping them assist co-ops not just in the "hardware" of collective production—technology, marketing, and so on—but in the "software" as well, including organizational format, institutional design, and political mediation.

It is striking that, despite their prior negative experience with co-ops (the large-scale, traditional Cooperativa Ensenada in the case of the fishermen, and LEA in the case of the farmers), the producers analyzed in this study established new co-ops that, in principle if not in size, resembled their previous organizations. The evidence indicates that producers learned from their previous co-ops at least what *not* to do, incorporating these lessons into the institutional design of their new co-ops. Moreover, both the fishermen and farmers have allied with other co-ops and plan to extend and strengthen these alliances in the future. Therefore, their experiences suggest that (re)organizing former members of "bad" co-ops—and there are an increasing number of them—is far from hopeless. From this perspective, the cases of Mortera and VIC-TOR may offer important insight about how to transform bad co-ops into good ones.

To conclude, the empirical material analyzed in this chapter underscores the important role that co-ops could continue to play in promoting economic development and alleviating poverty in rural Mexico. The words of one of Mortera's fishermen vividly express this potential:

> [Some people say] that the Mexican sea urchin fishermen don't know what we're doing. And, yes, maybe some of us are not at a good level [of organization].... But then how come so many Mexicans have gone to Japan lately? Before, the Japanese came and bought our sea urchin at the shore as soon as we brought it down from the boat.... Now *we* put the product on *their* tables.... If we didn't know what we were doing, then how did we do it?...
>
> How come a fisherman that hardly reads and writes and doesn't wear a tie is making international deals? Because we *do* know what we are doing ... because our fishing units from 1989 to 1995 have achieved what the [traditional] cooperatives couldn't since 1939.... The Japanese know that; they respect our fishing units and therefore they treat us well.

References

Arredondo Gómez, Félix. 1994. "Análisis de redes productivas de la pesquería del erizo de mar (*Strongylocentrotus franciscanus*) en Baja California, México." Master's thesis, Universidad Autónoma de Baja California.

Attwood, D. M., and B. S. Baviskar. 1987. "Why Do Some Cooperatives Work But Not Others? A Comparative Analysis of Sugar Cooperatives in India," *Economic and Political Weekly* 22 (26): A-38–A-55.

Barber, Bernard. 1983. *The Logic and Limits of Trust.* New Brunswick, N.J.: Rutgers University Press.

Espinoza Arroyo, Alejandro. 1992. *Los Rosareños: memorias del nacimiento y vida de un pueblo bajacaliforniano 1774–1992.* Ensenada, Mexico: Sector Pesquero de El Rosario/Museo de Historia de Ensenada.

Fox, Jonathan. 1992. "Democratic Rural Development: Leadership Accountability in Regional Peasant Organizations," *Development and Change* 23: 209–44.

Granovetter, Mark S. 1973. "The Strength of Weak Ties," *American Journal of Sociology* 78 (6): 1360–80.

Luhmann, Niklas. 1988. "Familiarity, Confidence, Trust: Problems and Alternatives." In *Trust: Making and Breaking Cooperative Relations*, edited by Diego Gambetta. Oxford: Basil Blackwell.

Magaña Magaña, Reynaldo. 1994. "Asociación estratégica en el sector rural: una alternativa de organización agroindustrial." Master's thesis, Universidad Autónoma de Baja California.

North, Douglass. 1990. *Institutions, Institutional Change and Economic Performance.* Cambridge: Cambridge University Press.

Olson, Mancur. 1977. *The Logic of Collective Action. Public Goods and the Theory of Groups.* Cambridge, Mass.: Harvard University Press.

Payeiro Nayar, Julio S. 1982. "Estimación de la densidad y crecimiento del erizo rojo *Strongylocentrotus franciscanus* (Agassiz) para la zona de Santo Tomás, Baja California, México." Master's thesis, Universidad Autónoma de Baja California.

Schmitz, Hubert. 1996. "From Ascribed to Earned Trust in Exporting Clusters." Sussex: Institute of Development Studies, University of Sussex. Mimeo.

SEMARNAP (Secretaría de Medio Ambiente, Recursos Naturales y Pesca). 1995. *Análisis de la temporada de pesca 1993–1994 del erizo rojo Strongylocentrotus franciscanus, en Baja California.* Ensenada, Mexico: Centro Regional de Investigación Pesquera de Ensenada.

Telser, L. G. 1980. "A Theory of Self-Enforcing Agreements," *Journal of Business* 53 (1).

Tendler, Judith. 1988. "What to Think about Cooperatives: A Guide from Bolivia." In *Direct to the Poor: Grassroots Development in Latin America*, edited by Sheldon Annis and Peter Hakim. Boulder, Colo.: Lynne Rienner.

Wade, Robert. 1988. *Village Republics. Economic Conditions for Collective Action in South India.* Cambridge: Cambridge University Press.

Wells, Miriam J. 1982. "Political Mediation and Agricultural Cooperation: Strawberry Farms in California," *Economic Development and Cultural Change* 30 (January): 413–22.

———. 1981. "Success in Whose Terms? Evaluation of a Cooperative Farm," *Human Organization* 40 (3): 239–45.

Williamson, Oliver. 1985. *The Economic Institutions of Capitalism*. New York: Free Press.

6

Four Responses to Neoliberalism: Peasant Organizations in Western Mexico

Francisco Javier Guerrero Anaya

Throughout the 1980s and into the early 1990s, rural Mexico experienced a wave of efforts to reorganize peasant production. As a partial consequence of these efforts, the fight for grassroots control of agricultural production has now shifted to a new arena in which the contest is not just over who will control surpluses but also over the very principles that will shape the economic relationship between the producers of basic grains and the consumers of their agricultural products.

Changing times demand new forms of economic organization. This is evidenced in the radical restructuring of the relationship between the Mexican government and rural Mexican society, in which the government has abandoned its traditional role in directing the rural economy and regulating the sale of basic foodstuffs. Under the old system, campesinos growing basic grains got their production loans, crop insurance, and fertilizer and other inputs through government-run companies, which also usually marketed the crop. In most cases, these parastatals also specified what crops to plant and how, which technological packages to use, how much fertilizer to apply, and at what price to sell the crop. This excessive dependence on the federal government distorted the agricultural sector's position in the national economy, and it blocked meaningful participation by rural society in public policy making. By the late 1970s, however,

Translation by Patricia Rosas.

some rural voices began to question the government's role and to propose changes in the state–rural sector relationship.

The federal government, meanwhile, was also beginning to re-evaluate the relationship. Beginning in 1982, under President Miguel de la Madrid (1982–1988), the Mexican government began moving toward a new, neoliberal development model that featured economic liberalization and that privileged free market principles over state regulation of the economy. The neoliberal model required modifications to the country's rural development policies, including changes in Article 27 of the Mexican Constitution and the dismantling of the parastatal companies that serviced the rural sector.[1] This chapter explores how rural producer organizations in western Mexico, especially in the state of Jalisco, have adapted to these market-oriented reforms.

In Jalisco in recent years there has been a strong organizational impetus among the state's very productive growers of basic grains[2] that attests to their tremendous capacity to respond to the withdrawal of government-owned enterprises from the countryside. The closure of FERTIMEX (Fertilizantes Mexicanos, S.A. de C.V.), the fertilizer company owned and operated by the federal government, had an enormous impact on Jalisco's rural economy, where demand for fertilizer ranges between 300,000 and 400,000 tons per year and where many campesino organizations had depended on income garnered through fertilizer distribution franchises (FDFs) with FERTIMEX. When FERTIMEX was dismantled, producer organizations quickly came together in a common front to seek out alternatives through which they could retain their position in the fertilizer market.

The alternative they pursued was to establish their own regional-level association in 1991—the National Association of Distributors of Agricultural Inputs and Fertilizer in the Social Sector (Asociación Nacional de Distribuidores de Insumos y Fertilizantes del Sector Social, A.C.)—and to negotiate with FERTIMEX for recognition as FDFs. As a result of these efforts, in which the growers received support from the National Peasants' Confederation (CNC) and the Union of Autonomous Regional Peasant Organizations (UNORCA), fourteen organizations in western Mexico won recognition as FDFs. Their success was more than a victory to win recognition as fertilizer distribu-

---

[1] These included ANAGSA, the national insurance corporation serving the agricultural and cattle ranching sectors; and FERTIMEX, a government-owned fertilizer company.

[2] According to figures from the Ministry of Agriculture, Livestock, and Rural Development (SAGAR), in 1994 Jalisco produced 2,379,659 tons of grain (an average of 3,556 kg per hectare), 13 percent of Mexico's total output (the average yield per hectare nationally is 2,100 kg).

tors; it was also a victory over the state government of Jalisco, which supported the monopolization of the fertilizer sector by RUCACO, S.A., a company partially owned by the son of then acting governor Guillermo Cosío Vidaurri. In fact, the state government's involvement actually served to strengthen the unity among campesino organizations in the region. With this as background, we can turn to the four peasant organizations that are the primary focus of this chapter.

Overview of the Cases

The first of the organizations analyzed in this chapter is the Western Agricultural Marketing Company (COMAGRO), founded in March 1992 by sixteen campesino organizations from the states of Jalisco, Nayarit, and Michoacán. By bundling orders for fertilizer, COMAGRO can purchase fertilizer in bulk at a lower price domestically or even buy it in the international market. COMAGRO also trades in grains, primarily corn, selling in volume and thereby winning a better return for its members. The organization offers training and agricultural extension services, and also designs computer systems for improved administration and agricultural forecasting. Today it is the umbrella organization for twenty-eight cooperatives: twenty-one in Jalisco, three in Nayarit, two in Michoacán, and one each in Colima and Querétaro.

The second case is the Rural Cooperative Society El Grullo (Sociedad Cooperativa Rural de El Grullo, Jalisco), in existence for over twenty-three years. Most of its economic activity focuses on two market sectors: (1) household goods sold in supermarkets, and (2) fertilizers and other agricultural inputs distributed through a regional network of warehouses. It also markets corn. The Rural Cooperative Society, which was a founding member of COMAGRO, has over 2,500 members from the municipalities of El Grullo, Autlán, El Limón, and Unión de Tula, and more than half of them are housewives.

The third case is the Ejido Union of the Ex-Laguna de Magdalena (Unión de Ejidos de la Ex-Laguna de Magdalena), which had its beginnings in the mid–1970s in a struggle for irrigation projects to prevent the flooding of its agricultural lands. It was also a founding member of COMAGRO. It has a membership of approximately 2,200 people from eleven ejidos[3] in four municipalities (Magdalena, Antonio Escobedo, San Marcos, and Etzatlán, where the organization's

---

[3] The ejidos are Antonio Escobedo, Etzatlán, Estancia de Ayllones, La Guadalupe, La Masata, La Joya, Magdalena, Oblatos, San Pedro, Santa Rosalía, and Las Juntas.

headquarters are located). It has been a pioneer in fertilizer marketing for seventeen years and in corn marketing for nine years. It is notable for its solid administrative structure, which has given continuity to its programs.

The fourth and final case is the Independent Peasant Organization of Jalisco "Manuel Ramírez" (OCIJ), which had its beginnings in the Catholic Church's ecclesiastical base communities that appeared in the early 1980s. OCIJ became an official campesino organization in 1987 and was incorporated in 1992. As of 1997, it included 555 rural producers, 75 percent of whom were men. It has evolved to become an active participant in the region's financial, production inputs, and grain markets and a promoter of agricultural infrastructure. Since its founding, it has included a team of professionals who provide technical support and advice. In 1997, OCIJ was in the process of joining COMAGRO.

These four organizations have responded to the liberalization of grain and fertilizer markets in ways that enhanced their development and consolidation. COMAGRO, as an umbrella for the other three organizations, shares their aim of centralizing demand for agricultural inputs and responding to deregulation of grain markets by creating economies of scale. Following reforms to the fertilizer marketing system, the Rural Cooperative Society was able both to retain market share in its own region and to expand into neighboring regions when their respective local organizations failed to manage the challenges posed by deregulation. The Ejido Union was a pioneer in fertilizer and grain marketing and the driving force behind the formation of COMAGRO. Although OCIJ was never involved in the fertilizer business, like the other three organizations under study it saw the withdrawal of FERTIMEX as an opportunity rather than a threat. In short, all four organizations may be considered relative success stories.

As these and other campesino organizations in Jalisco have moved to fill the institutional vacuums left by deregulation and the dismantling of parastatals, new relationships have developed among producers, government, and other economic actors involved in basic agriculture. Interacting in a precarious equilibrium, these actors are guiding Jalisco's transition from state intervention to the growers' direct participation in the marketplace.

Today new types of alliances exist between private-sector suppliers of fertilizer and agricultural chemicals and organized campesino groups. For example, corn growers who have achieved economies of scale have been able to negotiate contracts with agro-industrial giants like MASECA that dominate the corn flour market. Spaces are opening up for negotiating these kind of agreements, and they are often actively supported by the state government and campesino organizations.[4] One example is the establishment of a state-level Committee for Grain Sales, which provides producers and agro-industrialists with networking opportunities and information about market trends, and has forged a preliminary agreement to establish a Mexican agricultural commodity exchange.

The remainder of thes chapter will examine the four campesino organizations in terms of their consolidation, their strategies for resolving conflicts or contradictions as they pursue their goals, their political position, and their concrete activities and achievements.

A Socially Responsible Intermediary: COMAGRO

In March 1992, campesino organizations in western Mexico founded COMAGRO in response to the dismantling of FERTIMEX, which for years had controlled the production, distribution, and sale of fertilizers in Mexico by awarding distribution and sales concessions to private companies and producer organizations. The impending liquidation of FERTIMEX brought changes in the terms the parastatal offered to its concession holders. For example, the company drastically reduced the points of sale for fertilizer. It no longer delivered fertilizer on consignment but only on agreement to pay within thirty days, and then only when guaranteed by letters of credit. Each distributor had to be certified by FERTIMEX as a "primary distribution center" (CDP), and it was the distributor who had to develop—and take the risks associated with—a secondary distribution network.

Producer associations in Jalisco responded by uniting with organizations in Morelos, Veracruz, Sinaloa, and Sonora to form a bloc that would qualify them as CDPs. Several factors favored COMAGRO and its member associations. The dismantling of FERTIMEX coincided with the creation of the federal-level National Fund for Solidarity Enterprises (FONAES), part of the Mexican government's "Ten-Point Plan to Bring Liberty and Justice to the Mexican Countryside," which was designed to mitigate the effects of the reforms to Article 27 (Encinas Rodríguez 1995). And COMAGRO's ability to develop strategies and mobilize campesinos, along with its access to professional

---

[4] The Mexican state had traditionally intervened in markets for basic foodstuffs in a way that essentially foreclosed the option of establishing a direct link between the producer and the agro-industrialist. For example, CONASUPO's intermediary role of buying and selling grain represented the best option for both the campesinos and the food-processing industry, because CONASUPO's guaranteed purchase price was the highest the producer could get and CONASUPO heavily subsidized the price at which it sold to the processing plants.

advisers, gave it the tools necessary to present viable project proposals to FONAES—and thus to take full advantage of federal government policies aimed at alleviating the negative effects of the reforms. Recognizing the need to maintain the autonomy of its member organizations, COMAGRO channeled FONAES financing directly to its member associations, rather than centralizing the funding under COMAGRO's own control. This process also guaranteed against any single member's poor performance having repercussions on the association as a whole.

Researchers have differed somewhat in their analyses of COMAGRO's role (see for example, De la Fuente and Morales 1996: 306; Rodríguez Gómez and Torres 1994). Yet all seem to agree that COMAGRO has assumed obligations that at times exceeded its capacity. Its ambitious mission statement suggests this weakness:

> [Our goal is] to promote pervasive and lasting rural development by strengthening the economic and social organization of campesinos in general, of each member in particular, and of COMAGRO as a whole; to achieve a level of profitability in the rural sector that will support a decent standard of living for all rural residents (COMAGRO 1994).

In essence, COMAGRO is a social-sector actor operating according to private-sector rules, a contradiction it seeks to resolve by promoting competitive marketing strategies. But this activity has engendered a second contradiction between the role of socially responsible market regulator and that of profitable commercial enterprise. For example, in 1996 COMAGRO's fertilizer business was divided into three equal parts supplying its member organizations, private-sector clients, and COMAGRO's own warehouses. COMAGRO's members severely criticized this move because it put COMAGRO in direct competition with its affiliated organizations. Moreover, COMAGRO gave preference to private companies over its own membership in 1996, when fertilizer was expensive and in short supply. The criticism from its membership provoked a reorientation of COMAGRO's priorities, with a renewed focus on increasing agricultural production to benefit the producer organization, though without renouncing COMAGRO's role as a seller of agricultural inputs.[5]

COMAGRO has been a strong promoter of social mobilization, particularly to protest the low prices paid to grain producers. Following

---

[5] This proposal appeared in a report—"COMAGRO in the Year 2000"—presented for approval to the administrative councils and assemblies of the member associations before being sent for ratification in a general convention.

the devaluation of the peso in 1994, the peso price paid to corn producers should have risen in order to remain on par with the corn price in the dollarized international market, but the Mexican government refused to raise corn prices. COMAGRO participated actively in campaigns throughout Mexico to protest the government's decision not to exploit the country's comparative advantage in grains following the change in the peso's exchange rate against the dollar.

In October 1996 there was a second round of demonstrations to protest the drop in international corn prices, in which the associations united under COMAGRO showed their strong mobilizational capacity. Their leading role in the protests highlighted the eroding strength of the local CNC and the National Confederation of Smallholders (CNPP), the traditional PRI–affiliated corporatist organizations for campesino representation.[6] The demonstrations also underscored the need for new mechanisms of sectoral coordination better able to respond to the pressures of international markets.

As noted, COMAGRO diverged somewhat from its mission during 1996; it has since tried to reenergize and redirect its activities in order to recover the legitimacy it lost as a result of its preferential policies toward private companies. It has promoted comprehensive support packages for rural producers that include inputs and services: loans, extension services, technology transfers to boost productivity, and credible contracts that assure growers they will be able to sell their crops. Basically, COMAGRO is trying to decrease uncertainty for everyone involved in the agricultural production chain while it supports small producers in their struggle to obtain a better price for their crops.[7]

COMAGRO's primary objective, then, is to increase rural incomes as a means of raising rural living standards. Other factors that contribute toward improved living standards include core home services, savings and loan associations, and a social safety net—all of which

---

[6] The National Action Party (PAN) currently controls the state government in Jalisco, and affiliation with the CNC or CNPP, which under the old corporatist model was a requirement for obtaining any of the government's supports to agriculture, has begun to decline.

[7] The combination of COMAGRO's market position; its relative ascendance among campesino organizations; its alliances with grain purchasers (especially MASECA) and suppliers of fertilizers, agrochemicals, and seeds; and its relationships with financial institutions serving the countryside (especially FIRA and Banco BITAL) is opening up the possibility of contract agriculture in corn, wheat, and sorghum. Although contract agriculture is not new in Mexico (it has been used in sugarcane and tobacco), great care must be taken to protect the campesinos' ability to participate in decision making, to ensure that all parties understand the rules of the game, and to negotiate under terms of reciprocal trust toward a win-win outcome.

are included in the Rural Producers' Comprehensive Service Centers (CISAs) being promoted by COMAGRO.[8]

COMAGRO's promotion of the CISAs requires a rethinking of the pact between COMAGRO and its member organizations, which recognizes the autonomy of each member to make its own marketing decisions and to govern its relations with its member base. COMAGRO hopes to convince its members that they can best make their voices heard, not in the microregions in which each has authority, but by combining and integrating their decision-making authority in a forceful COMAGRO in the broader regional arena.

It may be that COMAGRO will fail to convince its members of the benefits of tighter integration, and it may fail to achieve the consensus needed to implement the CISAs, but there is also a strong possibility that it will succeed. In their analysis of COMAGRO, Muñoz Rodríguez and Santoyo C. note:

> [Mexico's producers] have lost competitiveness because of fragmentation and a failure to specialize, as well as because of the aggressiveness of their competitors. Joining together in a single producer organization would bring synergy, facilitate economies of scale, improve market image, and professionalize the operation of the organization itself [COMAGRO]....
> This organization has pioneered new approaches, called for change before it is imposed from outside, and persevered despite shakeups in its leadership and despite the shortsightedness and uncertainty of government policies (Muñoz Rodríguez and Santoyo C. 1996: 236).

In order to understand why COMAGRO has recently changed its strategy in favor of greater centralization, one must examine the evolution of the organization's operational underpinnings. During 1992 and 1993, the resources to support COMAGRO's operations came from the lines of credit that its member organizations negotiated individually with the National Rural Credit Bank (BANRURAL) or with private banks. COMAGRO's role was to help its members develop project proposals and compile the documentation the banks required before lending working capital. This framework assured that each member organization had the funds to buy necessary inputs.

---

[8] The goal for the CISAs is to build on the successes that member associations have had in different arenas, such as the provision of household goods by the Rural Cooperative Society, and technology transfer and productivity gains promoted by Agroferretera de la Ciénega, S.A., which in only two years managed to double per-hectare corn yields and realize a profit far above the state average.

COMAGRO's purchasing committee bundled its members' orders, but each affiliated organization retained the right to determine how it marketed its fertilizer.

In 1993, COMAGRO imported fertilizer for the first time. Its member organizations financed this transaction by combining their working capital with borrowed money and financing from the international supplier, Mitsubishi. This arrangement continued until December 1994, when Mexico's currency devaluation raised the cost of imported fertilizer to prohibitive levels. COMAGRO's member organizations were soon in financial distress, and several went into bankruptcy.

During the two years that it imported fertilizer, COMAGRO antagonized Mexico's producers of nitrogen-based fertilizer, whose sales were hurt by the competition from abroad. But COMAGRO was able to draft an agreement in 1994 with another domestic company, FERTINAL, a producer of phosphorous-based fertilizer. Under the terms of this agreement, FERTINAL was to supply COMAGRO with fertilizer and COMAGRO pledged not to import phosphorous-based fertilizer. This accord, which modified COMAGRO's relationship with its member organizations because financing now came from FERTINAL via COMAGRO, was never formalized because some members failed to pay for fertilizer they received.

Throughout 1996, COMAGRO's operations were based on an agreement it negotiated with Agronitrogenados, a domestic manufacturer of fertilizer with high nitrogen content. Agronitrogenados sent fertilizer to COMAGRO on consignment and provided most of COMAGRO's members' working capital. However, COMAGRO failed to market all of the fertilizer it requested from Agronitrogenados.

The preceding description of COMAGRO's operations goes far toward explaining the organization's changing strategies. COMAGRO achieved its initial success thanks to its strategy of sharing financial support and marketing risks across its membership; one member's failure would not pull down the others. When COMAGRO assumed greater financial risks in its agreements with specific suppliers, its members sometimes failed, for a variety of reasons, to meet their commitments or the company overstocked. Both of these circumstances generated distrust between COMAGRO and its membership and between COMAGRO and its suppliers.

COMAGRO's success lies in its ability to raise rural producers' incomes, which, in turn, has given them the wherewithal to survive as agricultural producers. COMAGRO'S challenge now is to demonstrate that it can be self-sustaining, that the alliances it has forged will enable it to achieve its mission.[9] Under its new operating model, COMAGRO must be innovative in developing and implementing rules for an equitable sharing of benefits and of decision-making authority if it is to improve relations with its membership and respond effectively to a changing rural development arena.

Strengths and Limitations of a Micro-Regional Focus: The Rural Cooperative Society

Founded in November 1974 with only twenty-nine members, the Rural Cooperative Society El Grullo has become one of Jalisco's most important campesino organizations. It has a direct impact on the welfare of more than 1,500 families; and, by forcing competitors to offer consumer goods at lower prices, it also has an indirect impact on the cost of living regionwide.

The Rural Cooperative Society, which developed out of a 1950s Community Chest sponsored by the Catholic Church, has sold fertilizer since 1976. It won status as a primary distribution center from FERTIMEX in 1992, at which point it undertook a broad expansion of operations. Its efforts were facilitated by the fact that it was able, with COMAGRO support, to get National Solidarity Program (PRONASOL) capital through FONAES, while many other distributors lacked such funding and could not compete under free market conditions.

The Rural Cooperative Society currently assists producers in twelve municipalities around El Grullo, the organization's headquarters and the site of its supermarket.[10] It meets 80 percent of the microregion's fertilizer needs. It marketed more than 22,000 tons in 1994 and 1995; distribution problems in 1996 reduced that year's sales to 18,000 tons. The Rural Cooperative Society has built up a network of warehouses through agreements with ejidos or ejido unions to lend or rent their warehouses to the cooperative and staff them with members of the local population. When warehouse space is loaned, the cooperative takes responsibility for its maintenance and repair; in some cases, the cooperative pays the ejido a commission based on tons of fertilizer sold. The terms of the agreement vary by locale be-

---

[9] COMAGRO has allied with Mitsubishi to form the COMIT company, established to consolidate the fertilizer market by taking advantage of both companies' connections with producers, Mitsubishi's financial strength, and COMAGRO's distribution network and membership. A second objective is to establish alliances with CIBA-Agro and other agro-industrial companies.

[10] The twelve towns are Ayutla, Unión de Tula, Cocula, San Gabriel, Colotlan, Tenamaxtlan, Autlán, El Grullo, El Limón, Tonaya, La Huerta, and Casimiro Castillo.

cause each is designed to provide the most benefit to the local producers as well as to the cooperative.

To date, the benefits of fertilizer marketing through the Rural Cooperative Society have come in terms of price, quality, and access to this key agricultural input, as well as inclusion in new programs for obtaining fertilizer under PROCAMPO.[11] Some members claim that the sale of fertilizers has generated so much profit that it underwrites the costs of maintaining the supermarket, though in truth the supermarket is itself self-supporting.

The cooperative has extended its services to cover agrochemicals, seeds, veterinary medicines, soil analysis, laser-guided field leveling, and precision sowing. It makes equipment available to all regional producers who join the cooperative, a strategy that has increased its membership. This growing amalgam of business ventures has improved the region's standard of living through the sale of consumer products at reasonable prices and through rising returns to agriculture thanks to the producers' access to inputs and services on favorable terms. The Rural Cooperative Society El Grullo describes its mission in the following terms:

> To participate in the construction of an economy in solidarity, to enhance the economic, social, and cultural conditions of our members, their families, and the community in general, through shared participation, organization, and cooperation. In our search for the common good, [we] support regional development ("Informe de Actividades de la Sociedad Cooperativa Rural El Grullo 1995").

It is important to evaluate the level of integration the Rural Cooperative Society maintains with its members. Many of the campesinos who only purchase fertilizers and other agricultural supplies through the organization view it as just one more supplier. This points to the organization's need to widen its involvement in organizing processes and outreach in the region. The organization's influence is much more visible among the members who reside in El Grullo, who have

---

[11] The change in federal government policy on agricultural subsidies—from guaranteed prices to direct subsidies for producers based on the number of hectares cultivated (PROCAMPO)—made it possible for the organizations to market agricultural inputs. Under the new policies, a cooperative can enter into agreement with the government agency (that is, PROCAMPO) and the producer for advance delivery of fertilizer to the producer. The government agency guarantees payment for the fertilizer by delivering the subsidy directly to the organization. Thus the government agency is able to carry out its mission of improving agricultural production by allocating the producer's subsidy up front in the form of a much-needed agricultural input.

ready access to the soil analysis service and the laser equipment for field leveling, and this should be factored into any evaluation of the cooperative's achievements.

The cooperative's distribution network was reinforced by the acquisition in 1994 of the storage infrastructure that had belonged to National Storehouses (ANDSA).[12] ANDSA's warehouses in El Grullo, Autlán, La Huerta, and Unión de Tula may well provide the impetus for the cooperative to expand its reach.

It is also important to examine the interactions between the Rural Cooperative Society and the Community Chest, the second cooperative in El Grullo. To date, each has maintained its autonomy, even though more than 80 percent of their respective memberships overlap and each organization offers services to the other.[13] Both the Community Chest and the Rural Cooperative Society recognize that they have a basis for working together. On the one hand, saving, lending, and consumption activities share some common features. The same extends to agricultural activities, which the Rural Cooperative Society has supported by providing producers with inputs, services, and capital. But there are other areas for cooperation, including education, that might also benefit from a joining of forces. In this sense, a basic condition for gaining an improved market position is to project a well-defined image as a cooperative enterprise:

> Cooperatives are businesses. It is their relationship with their members that sets them apart and makes them unique.... By definition, their principal characteristic is their associative structure as a group of people who join together willingly to address their shared economic, social, and cultural needs and aspirations. The means by which they do this is as a business, hence the cooperative's identification as a business organization (Pacheco 1996: 5).

On the other hand, this same author notes:

> Cooperation among cooperatives is an increasingly common economic practice because of the urgent need to serve

---

[12] ANDSA, a government company, was slated to close in 1993, but closure was postponed because of the rebellion in Chiapas. In 1995 it began selling off its existing warehouse infrastructure in rural areas, and this was to be followed by the sale of collection centers in strategic urban areas. The Rural Cooperative Society purchased the rural warehouses, and land on which they stand, at a bargain price, giving the organization an additional 45,000 tons in storage capacity.

[13] The Rural Cooperative Society sells coupons to the Community Chest that Community Chest employees can exchange for merchandise, and the Community Chest administers some of the savings of the cooperative.

their memberships. This is specific to cooperatives, and it can confer a strong competitive advantage given the vast networks of cooperatives throughout the hemisphere and the world (Pacheco 1996: 13).

In regard to Pacheco's first statement, it is important to acknowledge that cooperative identity is the result of an ongoing educational process. The Community Chest and the Rural Cooperative Society have proposed the establishment of a jointly run university; success on this front would enhance the development of both organizations.

Given the present state of Mexican agriculture, it would be helpful to identify the common areas or links in the productive process where these two organizations could collaborate to bring about regional development based on cooperation, equity, a fair distribution of resources, autonomy, and a continuing commitment to the community. By combining their strengths, they could achieve a more competitive market position based on these values, which are already an integral part of each organization's identity.

As a direct participant in the agricultural inputs market, the Rural Cooperative Society El Grullo has fully penetrated the regional fertilizer market, as discussed above. One of its members has sat on COMAGRO's administrative council since 1993, yet not all Rural Cooperative Society purchases are made through COMAGRO, which raises the possibility of some tension between the Society's direct participation in the inputs market and its commercial links to COMAGRO.

COMAGRO's member organizations have been able to profit as the fertilizer market moved from state control to rapid deregulation—and disarray. However, in recent years the trend has been toward stabilization and increased competitiveness. New suppliers have appeared, and COMAGRO's competitors have sometimes offered lower prices or better terms. Because the Rural Cooperative Society is an excellent client, it is a target of new suppliers. It now purchases between 60 and 80 percent of its inputs through COMAGRO and the remainder from other sources. While this practice may run against the basic premise that sustains the Society—because COMAGRO itself, as a company representing campesino organizations, is based on cooperative action—it calls attention to the fact that COMAGRO must remain responsive to its members' needs.

Combined purchasing through COMAGRO presents the Rural Cooperative Society with an opportunity to assume a leadership position in the regional supply network. The challenge in taking such a monumental step would be to imbue COMAGRO, its members, and each individual producer with the values and beliefs that underlie cooperatives, their business practices, and the comparative advantage they confer. Making this quantitative leap from microregional cooperative to "cooperative of cooperatives" with a regional reach would also require a *qualitative* leap in vastly extending a strategy designed for a local population whose principles, beliefs, and values may differ from those that prevail in rural society in general.

From Appropriating the Production Process to Improving Productivity? The Ejido Union

The Ejido Union of the Ex-Laguna de Magdalena was founded in 1976 at the peak of agrarian organizing during the presidential administration of Luis Echeverría (1970–1976). As befits a traditional, government-sponsored organization, it was founded by a long-time politico, which meant that during its early development its objectives were those dictated from above: to keep the campesinos under political control, to collaborate with the Ministry of Agrarian Reform (SRA) in promoting government initiatives, and to serve as a political trampoline for its leadership.

In 1979, as the result of an initiative proposed by the assembly of delegates, the Ejido Union launched a project to market fertilizer and invited a leader from the Ejido of Santa Rosalía to take charge of the program. He achieved excellent results despite the adverse conditions that existed at the time for obtaining fertilizer (FERTIMEX was distributing fertilizer through a private company).

Based on the popular support that his success with the fertilizer program had won him, the leader from Santa Rosalía decided to challenge the incumbent president of the Ejido Union in elections scheduled for late 1979. He and his slate carried the elections and set about legitimating their authority by establishing consultative mechanisms for decision making, selecting a council of respected local leaders, and responding to the demands of their campesino base, even when this brought them into conflict with government agencies. Thus it was that during its second stage of development—from 1979 to 1986—the Ejido Union lobbied for irrigation projects to prevent flooding in the more than 3,000 hectares of the old lagoon of the Ex-Laguna de Magdalena; continued to distribute fertilizer; gained recognition in 1981 as an official FERTIMEX distributor; participated in successful demonstrations in 1983 for higher corn prices; and, toward the end of this period, began selling corn and controlling its price, a highly profitable business formerly dominated by middlemen.

The Ejido Union gained ground thanks in large part to its strategy of struggle and its capacity for social mobilization, and to its independent stance vis-à-vis the official corporatist organization, the CNC. The CNC and other government agencies saw the Ejido Union as a rebel organization, yet recognized that it responded to its membership and that its leadership could pose a strong challenge to the governmental institutions.

The Ejido Union entered its third stage of development at a time of socioeconomic and political change. This period included a cleansing of public institutions that was undertaken in response to campesino demands for control of their own development, and this influenced the path of the organization and coincided with a change in its leadership. Following elections in 1986, the leader who had served as president of the organization from 1979 to 1986, reluctant to fade into the background, succeeded in winning appointment as adviser to the new board of directors. His actions in this post well exceeded his authority; he even issued orders that contravened those of the newly elected leaders. The Ejido Union's new leaders (1986–1991) ultimately distanced themselves from the former president and, by collaborating with the existing management team, were able to move ahead.

At this same time, as noted above, government agencies were in the process of modifying their mode of interaction with campesino organizations. The Ejido Union was able to capitalize on the changing landscape to maximize its proactive stance vis-à-vis the government agencies and win government funding for its projects and proposals. Because they were developed locally, these projects addressed issues that the Ejido Union deemed most relevant, and they were all directed at redressing the rural producers' disadvantaged position in the marketplace. As Gustavo Gordillo noted:

> It is important to determine what might be the fundamental components of a policy that enables ejidos to have their own base for accumulation. Taking the experience of the Coalición de Ejidos Colectivos de los Valles del Yaqui y del Maya as a guide, we can identify three such components: technical autonomy, financial autonomy, and market autonomy (Gordillo de Anda 1988: 45–46).

In the case of the Ejido Union, these three elements manifested themselves in distinct ways. Regarding financial autonomy, the Ejido Union was never able to establish its own credit institution. Yet when FERTIMEX altered its system for distributing fertilizer, the Ejido Union did develop a strategy designed to capitalize on this change.

> In 1990, the Ejido Union pressured to become part of the primary distribution network.... Later, it faced the virtually insoluble problem of providing the letters of credit that FERTIMEX was demanding before it would deliver fertilizer; the bank was requiring guarantees before it would estab-

lish a credit line, and the Ejido Union could not provide them. After intense discussion, the Ejido Union's administrative council and director developed an ingenious strategy that proved highly successful.... They asked the membership to entrust to the leadership the deeds and receipts for all their assets: machinery, tractors, threshing machines, houses, landholdings, livestock, pumping equipment, and so forth. A mountain of these documents was then delivered as collateral to the amused and surprised bank officials, who ultimately were convinced of the Ejido Union's determination to continue the fertilizer distribution program (Muñoz Rodríguez and Santoyo C. 1993: 2–3).

This anecdote attests to the solidarity among the Ejido Union's members and to their confidence in the leadership. Although it lacked a credit agency of its own, the Ejido Union demonstrated that it had other options in its search for credit and that it enjoyed a very high level of support and confidence among its members.

Besides distributing fertilizer, the Ejido Union began marketing corn in 1987 with the goal of increasing sales, getting a better price, and winning better terms of payment than traditional middlemen and the government's food distribution company (CONASUPO) formerly had provided. The Ejido Union regulated the market for corn on the cob, which does not fall under government price controls, and they implemented and operated a new subsidy program—the Support Program for Ejido Marketing, or PACE—funded by CONASUPO that supported threshing and transport to market. They established a PACE collective to extend the benefits of the program and to support the administration of marketing efforts and the creation and development of marketing infrastructure (with more than 700,000 pesos in government support from 1989 to 1992). And in 1994 the Ejido Union received funding to construct two mechanized silos with a capacity of 5,000 tons of grain.

In the area of technical autonomy, the case of the Ejido Union suggests that the inclusion of trained professionals is essential if campesino organizations are to become effective business operations. A professional staff can handle interactions with government agencies, support the efficient administration of operations, and identify new commercial opportunities. Another essential ingredient is continuity in projects and programs, which are vulnerable to the three-year terms of the Ejido Union's administrative council. The challenge is to reverse the mentality of "the new broom sweeps clean" that comes to the fore when an entering administration points to the mistakes of the preceding leadership and promises that it has new and better ideas.

According to researchers at the University of Chapingo, the Ejido Union has been effective on both counts:

> Over several years, the Ejido Union has assembled a technical team that handles much of the programmatic design, implementation, and operation and advises on important economic issues. This team presents alternatives and identifies the options that it considers optimal for the organization's projects.
>
> The fact that the technical team is directed by Antonio Hernández, who has also served as director of the Ejido Union since 1981, has brought continuity to the organization despite the successive leaderships' varying political perspectives and organizational programs. Thus, not only has the technical team been involved in the Ejido Union's administrative, financial, and commercial functions, but, under its experienced leadership, it has also been able to better coordinate its economic programs and initiatives (Morales Valderrama et al. 1996: 74–75).

This discussion confirms that the Ejido Union has achieved a measure of commercial success. Nevertheless, it is now torn between conflicting objectives: whether to continue as an important player in the grain and agricultural inputs markets or to seek a leadership role in the small producers' struggle to promote and manage a program to raise agricultural productivity. There are also tensions over competing uses for accumulated surpluses, which could be spent on modern warehousing infrastructure or, alternatively, for disseminating modern agricultural production techniques.

To date, the Ejido Union has tended to focus on how best to get crops into the market and on channeling government subsidies to resolve marketing problems. The measure of an organization's success traditionally has been the amount of funding it wins from the state and/or the amount of ground gained in its interactions with parastatal companies (like CONASUPO, FERTIMEX, BANRURAL, and so on), whether through political influence or through social mobilization. But the goals of producer organizations are evolving in the face of changing circumstances. BANRURAL has cut its lending for primary production dramatically, FERTIMEX no longer exists, and CONASUPO is no longer the best marketing option. Will it fall to producer organizations to fill the gap left by the government? In this new context, what producer needs can a producer organization reasonably fulfill, and what capacity do these organizations have with which to accomplish this?

Generally speaking, the Ejido Union's response has been confined to the marketing arena, and it has largely overlooked the whole set of

issues related to low agricultural productivity. This explains its focus
on the construction of modern warehouse infrastructure which offers
better marketing prospects and gives producers some protection
against price fluctuations.

> From the producers' perspective, the Ejido Union has
> played an important role at each moment of its evolution.
> In its initial phase, it catalyzed social action to demand that
> the government drain the lagoon. Later, it coalesced the
> growers' discontent over the government's guarantee
> prices. Then it played a critical part in the campesinos' en-
> try into fertilizer and corn marketing. This latter role be-
> came especially important when the Ejido Union began
> acting to regulate markets, just as the state was shedding
> its role as regulator of the agricultural sector (and this, in
> turn, helps explain the withdrawal of private brokers from
> the local market). But the organization's inherent limita-
> tions were visible; its achievements were neither stable
> (because the Ejido Union was itself immersed in a transi-
> tion toward economic consolidation) nor definitive. Thus it
> was that, in a moment of relative weakness within the
> Ejido Union and in the context of an attractive market, the
> agricultural brokers and middlemen appeared on the scene
> once more (Morales Valderrama et al. 1996, 128–29).

The Ejido Union has pioneered in introducing novel programs of
benefit to the rural economy. Yet the Ejido Union has not taken concrete steps in recent years to increase agricultural productivity, as
regional organizations have done elsewhere in Mexico.[14] And in this
regard, it has failed to develop a competitive advantage for its members. If the Ejido Union is to succeed as an enterprise whose primary
objective is to support rural development, it must successfully address a number of problems: the distancing of the leadership from its
base, the disarticulation of the ejido as a unit of production, the social
inequality among the ejidatarios themselves, the decapitalization of
agricultural producers, and the Ejido Union's own financial situation.
These problems do not excuse the organization from working toward
its founding goal. In fact, they require the Ejido Union to reaffirm its
initial mission:

---

[14] Such is the case with Agroferretera de la Ciénega, S.A. (see note 8). The Ejido Union
has succeeded in gaining similar support through official programs, and during 1993
and 1994 it participated in a regional economic stimulus program. It also has a laboratory for soil analysis, but this has been out of operation for years. The Ejido Union has
generally invested little in technical assistance to producers.

> To seek the growth and solidarity of our organization for the benefit of our members, fostering the perpetuation of the agricultural sector and the preservation of the environment. And, equally, to create an organization empowered to address changing circumstances and dedicated to promoting a fair standard of living for the rural population. This is to be achieved by organizing ourselves, the weak, to make us strong, promoting increased production and productivity, raising the returns to agricultural labor, and collaborating with other like-minded organizations.

Perspectives that envision peasant organizations that are active in the market merely as price regulators, or that see these organizations as entities to represent the rural sector in negotiations with the state or as catalysts to spark social mobilization, often fail to see that these organizations should operate as enterprises, which implies being competitive, professional, knowledgeable of clients' needs, demanding of suppliers, and always attentive to changing circumstances in order to discern new opportunities.

Challenges Facing the Ejido Union

The Ejido Union currently faces daunting challenges. As one group of researchers has noted:

> The social composition of the region is changing rapidly. Polarization and inequality are increasing among ejidatarios as the direct link between land and use rights is weakening. In recent years, there has emerged a small group of ejidatarios who concentrate land use, and even land ownership. These individuals often cultivate up to 100 hectares, and sometimes even more if land is combined and worked jointly by extended family groups. This trend is leading toward steadily increasing concentration in the region's agricultural production (Morales et al. 1996: 129).

Morales et al. note that the consolidation of the Ejido Union has not led to a decrease in social inequality among its members, nor has it diminished the sizable number of ejidatarios who are abandoning production. The authors call this the "erosion of the Ejido Union's traditional social base" (1996: 130); yet this process could also be interpreted as a trend toward greater market segmentation, with each segment requiring the development of different market strategies which, in turn, places more pressure on the organization for adaptability and flexibility in its daily operations.

It is important to note that the companies currently competing with the Ejido Union in the fertilizer market are challenging for market share among ejidatarios who have assembled production units of between 50 and 100 hectares (compared to a regional average of less than 6 hectares). This emphasizes the need for the Ejido Union's leadership to gauge the regional socioeconomic context (as well as the social differentiation to which it gives rise) on an ongoing basis in order to mitigate negative impacts and to envision necessary market adaptations.

Another major challenge to the Ejido Union involves cross-generational change. Many of the children of the original ejidatarios are better educated than their aging parents. And the ejidos can no longer absorb the diverse workforce—comprising these sons and daughters of ejidatarios, along with non-ejidatarios, day-laborers, manual workers, and service workers—that forms the population of rural ejidal communities. The Ejido Union had the vision to address the need for employment by pioneering in commercial enterprises, even if it failed to address the issue of agricultural productivity.

Nevertheless, the Ejido Union's mission must be examined critically by all of its members if the organization is to move from discussion to practice, and from practice to a shared ideology and identity. For this to occur, the organization must find a healthy and reasonable equilibrium between employment generation, infrastructure investments, and the delivery of complementary services that the ejidatarios need in order to increase the profitability of their land.

Combining Partisanship with Rural Development: The OCIJ "Manuel Ramírez"

The Independent Peasant Organization of Jalisco "Manuel Ramírez" (OCIJ) arose in Cuquio, Jalisco, growing out of the upsurge of ecclesiastical base communities in the early 1980s. Its geographic region is characterized by deep religious traditionalism and entrenched structures of power tightly linked to the central government and its structures of political control.[15]

---

[15] Local political power has long been in the hands of the González Quezada family, which has ties to both the state and federal power structures (an uncle is former governor of Jalisco, and another family member was in the upper echelons of the National Confederation of Smallholders [CNPP]). Moreover, the town of Cuquio is located in Los Altos de Jalisco, once a hotbed of the Cristero Rebellion and an area in which private ownership dominates ejidal land tenure.

Internal contradictions within the Catholic Church played a key role in the OCIJ's development. As the ideas and actions of liberation theology spread throughout Latin America (and within the Church itself), they gave rise to networks of exchange and mutual support among liberation theology's proponents. These networks included the Jesuits and laymen who, from the OCIJ's very beginnings, gave the organization their support and counsel and put its members in contact with the ecclesiastical base communities.

Key elements in the emergence, consolidation, and evolution of the OCIJ include the participation of the clergy, the organization's outreach to lay activists professing liberation theology, and its commitment to education as a means of promoting democratic participation based on shared principles and values. The OCIJ was launched in October 1987 in order to coordinate the efforts of all of Cuquio's poor campesinos to resolve the social and production problems of the local rural sector. During its first year, it promoted programs for production alternatives, improvements in public health through traditional medicine, recognition of agrarian rights in two communities, and, most importantly, public services, especially potable water and roads between communities. The OCIJ's tactics included demonstrations, takeovers of government offices, and marches to the municipal seat.

In 1988 the OCIJ joined the broad fight for democracy. It participated actively in opposition politics through the Unidad Popular, supporting candidate Rosario Ibarra de Piedra for the federal Congress and Cuauhtémoc Cárdenas for president. In December 1988 the OCIJ ran its own candidate for a seat in the municipal government and won. During this period, the organization was also supporting the creation of microenterprises, including sandal manufacture, small-scale pig farming, and apiculture, training campesinos in the necessary skills and making them self-sufficient in these activities. In this initial phase (1987–1988), the OCIJ was characterized by an ongoing process of mobilizations: in demand of public services, democracy, and agrarian rights.

From 1989 to 1992, the emphasis shifted to politics, including contesting for power within the municipality by building on the 1988 election of an OCIJ candidate; cementing its alliance with the Party of the Democratic Revolution (PRD); and participating in the 1992 municipal elections, in which the OCIJ won the municipal presidency.

The stronger emphasis on politics did not restrict the organization's activities in the social and economic arenas, however. The OCIJ worked with women's groups, started a lending program supported by nongovernmental organizations, and pursued a struggle for land that resulted, in 1988, in the extension of the Ocotic ejido (adding 400 hectares allocated among 90 ejidatarios). From 1993 to 1996, the organization focused on the campesinos' economic organization and on participatory decision making on issues of municipal development (from 1992 to 1995, Cuquio was the only municipality in Jalisco controlled by the PRD).[16] In its efforts to improve social well-being, in 1996 the OCIJ sought the support of the federal Ministry of Social Development (SEDESOL) for a housing program that would benefit 122 families in five communities. The repayment of the loans made to campesinos under this program were to enter a permanent revolving fund to capitalize housing construction.

The organization's economic focus led it to develop other significant programs. One involves financing for growers of corn and tomatillo, through which OCIJ established a trust fund to help offset the risk of agricultural ventures. In 1996 this program extended credit to cover 5,000 hectares at an average of 1,780 pesos per hectare. The program is officially part of the Investment Funds for Rural Development (FINCA), which includes crop insurance, a contingency fund, and a capitalization fund, all aimed at reducing the risks of agricultural production. Since 1993 the OCIJ has also operated a system of "on-your-honor" loans that financed production on more than 800 hectares. This program is remarkable in that it has achieved a 100 percent rate of repayment. Monies paid back into the fund support public works chosen by the community, including, to date, a consumers' cooperative with outlets in four communities (Cuquio, La Esperanza, Juchitlán, and Ocotic).

A second OCIJ program involves the distribution of fertilizers and other agricultural inputs. Begun in 1993, it quickly wrested market share from its (less than honest) competitors, who sold underweight "50 kilo" bags and adulterated their fertilizer with dirt. In 1996, the OCIJ program sold 5,000 tons of fertilizer and more than 2 million pesos worth of seeds and agrochemicals, supplying more than 50 percent of the regional market. The fertilizer program has taken extensive advantage of PROCAMPO, which assures a speedy delivery of funding for production and promotes an efficient use of inputs. During 1996, 2,000 hectares in the region were covered by the PROCAMPO program, and local producers received a credit line of one million pesos from PROCAMPO. In addition, the OCIJ is one of few organizations accredited by BANRURAL, from which it obtained a credit of 2,700,000 pesos.

The third OCIJ program, for corn marketing, began with the 1994–95 harvest, when the organization marketed 5,000 tons of corn. By

---

[16] Within the municipal government, the OCIJ established a decision-making entity, the Municipal Democratic Committee (CODEMUN), in which representatives from different communities analyzed, debated, and selected priority public projects.

1996–97, the amount had risen to direct sales of 14,000 tons, and 3,000 tons sold in conjunction with the municipal government. Together this represents 75 percent of the corn traded in the municipality. The corn program also received a credit line from BANRURAL similar to that of the fertilizer program.

A fourth program went into effect at the end of 1993, with the endorsement and funding of a foreign foundation. This was the program for developing production and marketing infrastructure. The purchase of a small bulldozer enabled the OCIJ to undertake small infrastructure projects, whose beneficiaries covered operating costs and loan amortization. Projects completed thus far include ninety dirt dikes whose reservoirs can hold approximately 900 m^3 of water; more than 10 km of farm roads; and two warehouses with grain scales (constructed with additional support from the state government). The success of the infrastructure program speaks to the mobilizing power of social-sector enterprises and their ability to make good use of governmental and nongovernmental support through democratic decision making, transparency, and good relations with other institutions.

Its integration into the economic-commercial dynamic has led the OCIJ to redefine its membership, which initially included only poor campesinos. Today, the organization also includes wealthier, commercial producers. According to the OCIJ mission statement, the organization's goal is to "promote the socioeconomic organization of the region's producers in ways that benefit and involve families, the community, and the OCIJ in the pursuit of a decent standard of living for both poor campesinos and commercial producers."

The OCIJ has already achieved a high degree of technical, financial, commercial, and (especially) organizational autonomy. It has formed twenty-four rural production societies, and three more are on the way, each with representative, executive, and technical units. Although each rural production society is autonomous, with its own leadership, each one also coordinates activities with the others, creating a point of intersection at which the general organization of the OCIJ can provide assistance and/or direction. One risk that the OCIJ may be running is an overcentralization of operations, which limits the size of the population from which it draws its leadership and leads to an overdependence on a small cohort of individuals.

The causes for which the OCIJ has advocated have brought it into a series of confrontations with the regional power elite. For example, in 1988 municipal officials and ultraconservative families in Cuquío pressured for removal of the parish priest. He was replaced by a conservative curate who rejected the work of the ecclesiastical base communities and promoted the formation of alternative religious groups. He also publicly repudiated the work of the OCIJ and halted the pastoral efforts of the Jesuits. This confrontation effectively reduced the number of community members who dared question the status quo, and it strengthened the traditional power group's position in the municipality. Nevertheless, the impetus that the Jesuit clergy gave the OCIJ in its earliest days could not be revoked; and it provided an important institutional mantle during the organization's embryonic stage, enabling the OCIJ to become the powerful and autonomous peasant and popular organization that it is today.

It is important to note that the establishment of the OCIJ was also made possible by the reforms to Mexico's agrarian law that supported associational forms that are not subject to ejidal authority. The ejido form of land tenure developed as a means of assuring the social sector's access to land. Yet rather than promoting campesino self-government, the legal institution underlying the ejido structure became a tool by which the federal government could exert political and social control over rural producers. This gave rise to *caciquismo ejidal*, in which rural bosses exercised power based on a network of patron-client relationships. In this system, the ultimate patron was the federal government, which granted the campesinos access to land but denied them a role in decision making on the very economic and social policies that governed their lives, placing this authority instead in the hands of the ejido governing bodies.

As the ejido came to be seen as a mechanism for controlling the countryside, its original purpose was lost from view. People forgot that the ejido was intended to be a viable unit of production, not just an arena for subsistence agriculture. Thus the ejido's ability to mobilize production was allowed to atrophy, and its social energy and productive role were submerged beneath its role as guarantor of political control in the countryside. In effect, the ejido became a reserve army of cheap labor.

The OCIJ began on the assumption that the political subordination of the campesino had to end and that new spaces had to be opened for the campesinos' economic participation. Paradoxically, it found support in the reforms to Article 27 of the Mexican Constitution, which defined a new legal framework for granting greater associational autonomy to rural producers (especially in the ejido sector) via rural production societies.

In short, the OCIJ is the culmination of an organizational process that derived from social mobilizations and evolved into a strong and effective proponent of autonomy and democracy in all spheres of rural life—social, economic, and political. It has developed its own ideology and disseminated it among its membership. It has developed a flexible organizational culture that is responsive to socioeconomic change. And it has not lost sight of its mandate to mold the socioeconomic context to favor its membership.

Conclusion

The campesino organizations studied here have responded in varied ways to the challenges posed by neoliberal policy reform. COMAGRO is reorienting its priorities toward increasing agricultural productivity and thus raising the living standard of rural producers, in line with its primary goal of bringing dignity to Mexico's campesino population. The Rural Cooperative Society El Grullo intends to expand regionally, based on disseminating the principles of cooperativism and mutual support as the articulating axis of organization; this expansion includes the creation of a cooperative university. The Ejido Union of the Ex-Laguna de Magdalena faces the challenge of redefining its strategies for serving rural producers in response to the social differentiation that is occurring in the region. The OCIJ, meanwhile, plans to continue its participation in several arenas, including financing basic agriculture, providing inputs and extension services, and marketing production. At the same time, it seeks to promote social well-being through its consumer cooperative and housing program, and by encouraging the formation of rural production societies that can free rural producers from the control of power bosses in the ejidos.[17]

Mexico's campesinos now face multiple challenges: to participate in the market as strong and adequately capitalized competitors; to increase output; to raise rural living conditions through social mobilization and democracy; and to forge relations based on justice and equality in their interactions with other actors in the agro-food chain. To manage these tasks, campesino organizations must demonstrate several specific qualities. The first characteristic combines two elements: (1) preservation of the grassroots principles, values, and beliefs that together form a central ideology shared throughout the organization; and (2) the creativity, effectiveness, and flexibility needed to design and implement strategies tailored to members' demands and changing economic conditions, strategies that channel organizational activities toward constructing a vision of a stable future based on participatory planning and decision making.

The second essential characteristic is multifunctionality. The campesino organizations studied here are, simultaneously, social-sector enterprises, catalysts of social mobilization, power centers that offer campesinos an opportunity to participate in democratization at the

---

[17] It is important to note that the new organizational forms emerging in rural Jalisco—even though they do not fully contradict the authority of the ejido—clearly demonstrate that the ejido is no longer as relevant as it was in the past. This is not surprising; the ejido came into being so that the state could regulate access to land, yet no more land will be distributed in the future.

municipal and federal levels, and ideological wellsprings in support
of campesinos' social and cultural inclusion. Their multiple roles imply multiple responsibilities: to regulate markets for agricultural inputs and output; to provide services to campesinos; to influence public policy; and to open up government planning agencies. Like the
first characteristic outlined above, which combines the components of
ideology and flexibility, the characteristic of multifunctionality also
aims to increase campesinos' market competitiveness and to influence
rural development in ways that include campesinos as valid actors.

A final key characteristic of organizations is the need for effective
coordination between their leadership and their highly professional-
ized technical and administrative teams. All four case studies analyzed here have achieved a clear division of responsibilities. In each
instance, the leadership sets the course, makes strategic decisions,
approves operational plans, heeds the demands of the organization's
grassroots base, and establishes and maintains outreach to key public
and private institutions. The technical and administrative staff pro-
poses and implements strategies approved by the leadership, gener-
ates and analyzes information, manages day-to-day operations, and
provides program continuity.

Campesino organizations that combine these various qualities will
have a firm basis for overcoming the challenges posed by Mexico's
neoliberal reforms.

References

De la Fuente, Juan, and Joaquín Morales. 1996. "Crisis rural y respuesta cam-
pesina: la Comercializadora Agropecuaria de Occidente." In *Neoliberal-
ismo y organización social en el campo mexicano*, edited by Hubert C. de
Grammont. Mexico: Plaza y Valdés.
Encinas Rodríguez, Alejandro, ed. 1995. *El campo mexicano en el umbral del
Siglo XXI*. Mexico: Espasa Calpe.
Gordillo de Anda, Gustavo. 1988. *Estado, mercados y movimiento campesino*.
Mexico: Plaza y Valdés/Universidad Autónoma de Zacatecas.
Morales Valderrama, Joaquín, et al. 1996. "La Unión de Ejidos General
Lázaro Cárdenas de la Ex-Laguna de Magdalena, Jalisco." Mimeo.
Muñoz Rodríguez, Manrubio, and V. Horacio Santoyo C. 1993. "Unión de
Ejidos "Mario Moreno" Agronegocios." Texcoco, Mexico. Mimeo.
———. 1996. *Visión y misión agroempresarial. Competencia y cooperación en el
medio rural*. 2d ed. Mexico: Universidad Autónoma de Chapingo.
Pacheco, Juan Diego. 1996. "Declaración de identidad cooperativa." Pre-
sented at the Sixth Congreso Nacional de Cajas Populares. Mimeo.
Rodríguez Gómez, Guadalupe, and Gabriel Torres. 1994. "El Barzón y Comagro: dos estrategias frente a la modernización neoliberal del campo," *Revista Cuadernos Agrarios*, año 4, no. 10.

Acronyms

ANAGSA	Aseguradora Nacional Agrícola y Ganadera, S.A. / National Agricultural and Livestock Insurance Agency
ANDSA	Almacenes Nacionales de Depósito, S.A. / National Storehouses
ARIC	Asociación Rural de Interés Colectivo / Rural Collective Interest Association
BANCOMEXT	Banco de Comercio Exterior
BANRURAL	Banco Nacional de Crédito Rural / National Rural Credit Bank
CCI	Centro Coordinador Indigenista / Indigenous Coordinating Center
CDP	*centro de distribución primaria* / primary distribution center
CEPCO	Coordinadora Estatal de Productores de Café de Oaxaca / Statewide Coordinating Network of Coffee Producers of Oaxaca
Cigatam	Cigarrera La Tabacalera Mexicana
CIOAC	Central Independiente de Obreros Agrícolas y Campesinos / Independent Central of Agricultural Workers and Peasants
CISA	Centro Integral de Servicio al Agricultor / Rural Producers' Comprehensive Service Center
CNC	Confederación Nacional Campesina / National Peasants' Confederation
CNOC	Coordinadora Nacional de Organizaciones Cafetaleras / National Coordinating Network of Coffee Producers' Organizations
CNPP	Confederación Nacional de Pequeños Propietarios / National Confederation of Smallholders
CNPR	Confederación Nacional de Propietarios Rurales / National Confederation of Rural Smallholders

CODEMUN	Comité Democrático Municipal / Municipal Democratic Committee
COMAGRO	Comercializadora Agropecuaria de Occidente, S.A. / Western Agricultural Marketing Company
CONASUPO	Compañía Nacional de Subsistencias Populares / National Subsidized Staple Products Company
COPLADE	Comité de Planeación para el Desarrollo del Estado / State Planning Commission
CTM	Confederación de Trabajadores de México / Confederation of Mexican Workers
FDT	Frente de Defensa Tabaquero / Front for the Defense of Tobacco Growers
FERTIMEX	Fertilizantes Mexicanos, S.A. de C.V.
FIDECAFE	Fideicomiso del Café / National Coffee Trust Fund
FINCA	Fondos de Inversión para el Desarrollo Rural / Investment Funds for Rural Development
FIRA	Fideicomiso Instituido en Relación con la Agricultura / Agricultural Trust Fund
FIRCO	Fideicomiso de Riesgo Compartido / Trust Fund for Shared Risk
FONAES	Fondo Nacional de Empresas de Solidaridad / National Fund for Solidarity Enterprises
FRS	Fondos Regionales de Solidaridad / Regional Solidarity Funds
FUPPE	Federación de Unidades Productivas Pesqueras Ejidales / Federation of Ejido Fishing Production Units
ICO	International Coffee Organization
IMSS	Instituto Mexicano del Seguro Social / Mexican Social Security Institute
INI	Instituto Nacional Indigenista / National Indigenous Institute
INMECAFÉ	Instituto Mexicano del Café / Mexican Coffee Institute
ITAO	Instituto Tecnológico Autónomo de Oaxaca / Autonomous Technological Institute of Oaxaca
NAFTA	North American Free Trade Agreement
OCIJ	Organización Campesina Independiente de Jalisco "Manuel Ramírez," S.C. / Independent

	Peasant Organization of Jalisco "Manuel Ramírez"
ORMICH	Organización de Mujeres Chatinas / Organization of Chatino Women
PACE	Programa de Apoyo a la Comercialización Ejidal / Support Program for Ejido Marketing
PAN	Partido Acción Nacional / National Action Party
PRD	Partido de la Revolución Democrática / Party of the Democratic Revolution
PRI	Partido Revolucionario Institucional / Institutional Revolutionary Party
PROCAMPO	Programa de Apoyo Directo al Campo / Direct Rural Support Program
PRONASOL	Programa Nacional de Solidaridad / National Solidarity Program
PT	Partido del Trabajo / Labor Party
SAGAR	Secretaría de Agricultura, Ganadería y Desarrollo Rural / Ministry of Agriculture, Livestock, and Rural Development
SAM	Sistema Alimentario Mexicano / Mexican Food System
SARH	Secretaría de Agricultura y Recursos Hidráulicos / Ministry of Agriculture and Water Resources
SC	*sociedad civil* / civil association
SECOFI	Secretaría de Comercio y Fomento Industrial / Ministry of Commerce and Industrial Development
SEDESOL	Secretaría de Desarrollo Social / Ministry of Social Development
SEMARNAP	Secretaría de Medio Ambiente, Recursos Naturales y Pesca / Ministry of the Environment, Natural Resources, and Fisheries
SHCP	Secretaría de Hacienda y Crédito Público / Ministry of Finance
SNTE	Sistema Nacional de Trabajadores de la Educación / National Education Workers Union
SPR	*sociedad de producción rural* / rural production society
SSS	Sociedad de Solidaridad Social de los Productores de Tabaco del Estado de Chiapas / Social Solidarity Society of Tobacco Producers of Chiapas

TABAMEX	Tabacos Mexicanos, S.A. de C.V.
Tadesa	Tabacos Desvenados, S.A.
TERSA	Tabaco en Rama, S.A.
TPN	Tabacos del Pacífico Norte
UCI "Cien Años"	Unión de Comunidades Indígenas "Cien Años de Soledad" / Union of Indigenous Communities "One Hundred Years of Solitude"
UCIRI	Unión de Comunidades Indígenas de la Región del Istmo / Union of Indigenous Communities of the Isthmus
UCIZONI	Unión de Comunidades Indígenas de la Zona Norte del Istmo / Union of Indigenous Communities of the Northern Isthmus
UE	Unión de Ejidos/ Union of Ejidos
UEPC	Unidades Económicas de Producción y Comercialización / Economic Units for Production and Marketing
UEPRV	Unión de Ejidos Primitivo R. Valencia
UNAM	Universidad Nacional Autónoma de México / National Autonomous University of Mexico
UNORCA	Unión de Organizaciones Regionales Campesinas Autónomas / Union of Autonomous Regional Peasant Organizations
UNOSJO	Unión de Organizaciones de la Sierra Juárez de Oaxaca / Union of Organizations from the Sierra Juárez of Oaxaca
UOPICAFE	Unión de Organizaciones de Productores Indígenas de Café / Union of Indigenous Coffee Producers' Organizations
UPPE	*unidad de producción pesquera* / ejidal fishing production unit
WTO	World Trade Organization

About the Contributors

Francisco Javier Guerrero Anaya holds a degree in Communication from the Instituto Tecnológico y de Estudios Superiores de Occidente (ITESO) in Guadalajara. He has been active in campesino organizations since 1980 and currently serves as Director of Planning and Development with the Comercializadora Agropecuaria de Occidente, S.A. de C.V., in Guadalajara, Jalisco.

Jorge Hernández Díaz, a social anthropologist, is a Research Professor at the Instituto de Investigaciones Sociológicas of the Universidad Autónoma "Benito Juárez" de Oaxaca. He has written extensively on indigenous political affairs among the Trique, Zapotec, Huave, and Chatinos of southern Mexico. His publications include *El café amargo. Cambio y diferenciación social entre los chatinos* (UABJO, 1987), *Los chatinos: etnicidad y organización social* (Estado de Oaxaca/UABJO 1993); and "Bilingual Teachers: A New Indigenous Intelligentsia," in *The Politics of Ethnicity in Southern Mexico*, edited by Howard Campbell.

Horacio Mackinlay, a Professor at the Universidad Autónoma Metropolitana–Iztapalapa, is currently completing his doctorate in sociology at the Universidad Nacional Autónoma de México. His research interests include Mexico's legislative reforms, peasant movements, and agro-industry in the era of economic restructuring. He contrasts the situation in the Mexican countryside before and after the neoliberal property reforms of the early 1990s, with a special focus on the tobacco sector in Nayarit, Veracruz, and Chiapas. He is coauthor of "El movimiento campesino y las políticas de concertación y desincorporación de las empresas paraestatales" (with Juan de la Fuente), in *Campo y ciudad en una era de transición*, edited by Mario Bassols; and "La CNC y el nuevo movimiento campesino," in *Neoliberalismo y organización social en el campo mexicano*, edited by H. C. de Grammont.

Richard Snyder is Assistant Professor of Political Science at the University of Illinois, Urbana-Champaign. His publications include *The Future Role of the Ejido in Rural Mexico* (coedited with Gabriel Torres,

Center for U.S.–Mexican Studies, 1998); "After the State Withdraws: Neoliberalism and Subnational Authoritarian Regimes in Mexico," in *Subnational Politics and Democratization in Postrevolutionary Mexico*, edited by Wayne Cornelius, Todd Eisenstadt, and Jane Hindley; and *Strategies for Resource Management, Production, and Marketing in Rural Mexico* (coedited with Guadalupe Rodríguez, forthcoming). He is currently completing a book manuscript entitled "Politics after Neoliberalism: Reregulation in Mexico, 1985–1995."

Jorge Mario Soto Romero is a Ph.D. candidate in Urban Studies and Planning at the Massachusetts Institute of Technology. His academic interests focus on economic development and poverty alleviation in developing countries; his dissertation examines the role of development banking in Mexico's industrial growth.

Publication of important new research on Mexico and U.S.–Mexican relations is a major activity of the Center for U.S.–Mexican Studies. Statements of fact and opinion appearing in Center publications are the responsibility of the authors alone and do not imply endorsement by the Center for U.S.–Mexican Studies, the International Advisory Council, or the University of California.

For a list of all Center publications and ordering information, please contact:

Publications Sales Office
Center for U.S.–Mexican Studies
University of California, San Diego
9500 Gilman Drive, DEPT 0510
La Jolla, CA 92093-0510
Phone (858) 534-1160   Fax (858) 534-6447
e-mail: usmpubs@weber.ucsd.edu